# What People Are Saying About

For every aspect of management, there are a fe̶͟w̶ ... ̶ ̶o̶r the element of leadership, coaching is one of tho̶s̶e̶ ... book, Tom captures the full dimensionality of both the spirit and pra̶c̶t̶... ̶g̶.

**Jerrold R. Bratkovich, President & Chief Operating Officer**
**Organization Resources Counselors, Inc.**

This book broadens the role of leadership in organizations by effectively defining the multi-dimensional skill needed for success today and in the future.

This book should not be IN every executive's bookshelf; it belongs ON THE DESK as a just-in-time resource for high-impact coaching.

**Scott Tempel, Senior Consultant**
**PacifiCare Health Systems**

*The Heart of Coaching* arrives at the right time, when leaders need a vision to help them go beyond teamwork. This approach to Transformational Coaching places ownership for the problem where it belongs, with the person responsible for finding a solution. This is true empowerment.

**David M. Lehmann, Vice President & General Manager, Mfg.**
**Solar Turbines, Division of Caterpillar**

Tom Crane makes a compelling and passionate case that Transformational Coaching is THE REQUISITE SKILL for creating truly aligned and powerful organizations.

The book is full of information, tips, and models that help explain this significant art and skill.

**Robin Reid, Managing Partner**
**Reid, Moomaugh & Associates**

Today's marketplace demands that leaders place a renewed focus on coaching— the same attention as on strategy. Tom gives us valuable insight on precisely how to best coach others as we continue to strive for excellence throughout the workplace.

**Ronald J. Burns, President & Chief Operating Officer**
**Entergy Corporation**

*The Heart of Coaching* will touch your spirit and enable you to develop and sustain a consistently high-performance culture.

**Robert W. Best, Chairman, President, & C.E.O.**
**Atmos Energy Corporation**

Tom Crane has devoted much of his professional career to the art and practice of coaching. He has "walked a mile" in these moccasins. Here he offers a clear, accessible and proven guide for all leaders who are committed to deepening their coaching skills.

This book represents his "heart advice" to those of us who would call ourselves "coaches." Both wisdom and compassion are needed, and Tom's exploration of these themes is useful to the seasoned leader/manager, as well as to fellow practitioners of coaching from the heart.

**Timothy Smith, President**
**Wheelwright Associates**

*The Heart of Coaching* gives valuable insights for setting the right performance targets and effectively communicating for results. It shows us step by step how to use coaching to develop people and manage the process of change.

It is one of those books that we all wish we read 20 years ago because it would have made a world of difference in our own development as coaches.

**John A. Brady, Ph.D., President**
**Brady & Associates**

Managers and human resource professionals are increasingly being held accountable for making a difference in the performance of their people. This book is a highly practical, "hands-on" approach to managing human and organizational performance.

The models and methods are based on the solid integration of experience in a wide array of organizations. This book shows you how to generate strategically focused learning and get desired results through the development of the organization's most important resource—its people.

**John E. Jones, Ph.D., President**
**Organizational Universe Systems**

# The Heart of Coaching

## Using Transformational Coaching To Create a High-Performance Culture

### Thomas G. Crane

with Lerissa Patrick

FTA
PRESS

The Heart of Coaching:
Using Transformational Coaching to Create a High-Performance Culture

ISBN: 0-9660874-0-2
Library of Congress Catalog Card Number: 97-78150

Cover and interior by Troy Scott Parker, Cimarron Design
Printed in the United States of America
Printing, last digit: 9  8  7  6  5  4  3  2

Second printing, August 1998

Published by FTA Press
11052 Picaza Place
San Diego, California 92127
619/487-9017 phone
619/592-0689 fax

# Contents

# Dedication

My first coach was Hubert Hansel. He was my science and physical education teacher in seventh grade and coached my junior high school basketball team.

Since becoming a consultant and helping leaders to become coaches for their organizations, I have reflected on the effect my coaches had on me. It is clear that the beliefs and values on which I've constructed my life were articulated, taught, and strengthened on the basketball court by Coach Hansel. Although I've had many coaches since Coach Hansel, none so completely epitomized the essence for me of *who* a coach is.

I learned the following life principles from Coach Hansel, who served as a role model for them all:

- Be a good sport; play by the rules
- Practice the fundamentals; how you practice is how you play
- Give it your best effort; never hold back
- Commit to winning, but lose gracefully
- Work hard at getting better; you can always improve
- Cheer and support your teammates on and off the court
- Live life in a spiritual context with a purpose
- Be a role model; other people are watching you

I can track the successes I've had in my life back to these principles of life success. With sincere gratitude, I dedicate this book to Coach Hansel, for his unselfish giving and his commitment to bringing his heart and the best of *who* he is to the practice of coaching.

# Acknowledgments

According to African wisdom, "it takes a village to raise a child." Well, it took a team to finish this book. There are many people who contributed in very important ways to support me in this project. I wish to publicly thank them all here.

My numerous friends at Senn Delaney Leadership provided me coaching for my personal growth and an opportunity as a consultant to work on the human side of the enterprise. This is now my life's work.

Cathy Zaitzow helped me to create the original book outline as something coherent and potentially intelligible. Robin McLinden, Mary Jo Jenkins, and Anne Machen added their listening and word-processing skills to help me get the words down on paper.

Lerissa Patrick, as editor, helped to shape the book into its final form. Through our ongoing dialogue, she helped me to develop and refine the ideas I started with and to present them more gracefully than I ever could have on my own.

Many associates and colleagues added their constructive comments to the earlier drafts, helping me to look at the book from a readers perspective: Robin Reid, John Jones, David and Rebecca Grudermeyer, Scott Tempel, Lynn Ripplemeyer, Deb Fortune, Cheri Huber, C.O. Woody, Elizabeth Brown, Jim Sale, Alanna Roberts-Lal, and Maryellen Crane.

Rebecca Taff brought her keen eye in copy editing. Arlette Ballew added her considerable editing skills to polish the final presentation of the material. Troy Scott Parker added his creative talent in cover and interior design, further adding to the elegance of the Transformational Coaching model.

I received strong encouragement and emotional support from two special people. John Brady and Tim Smith have been role models for who a coach is and a constant source of inspiration to follow what was in my heart.

I would also like to acknowledge my kids, Andy, Jason, and Claire, for being in my life and for providing me lots of opportunities to grow as a parent and to transform myself into a more loving and accepting person. I am a better coach as a result.

Maggie, my life partner, has been my strongest teacher. She also has provided very substantive feedback on the writing and final revisions of the manuscript. I especially thank her for supporting me in realizing more of my potential as a caring human being capable of sharing this heartfelt approach to working with people.

# Introduction

What if people in your organization:

- Knew the mission of the business and their role in creating success?
- Knew the organizational priorities and acted with a sense of urgency?
- Were committed to give their personal best efforts and did not hold back because of fear of failure?
- Freely contributed to organizational goals without worrying about who got the credit?
- Consistently achieved the results they were capable of achieving?
- Valued one another's thoughts and ideas and treated their teammates with respect and compassion?
- Openly shared feedback with one another without fear of reprisal?
- Sought out and responded appropriately to performance feedback?
- Had fun at work?

These "what if's" are not pipe dreams but are conditions frequently found in high-performing teams. These teams are able to consistently outperform their rivals because their high-performance culture energizes and focuses people on the strategic goals of the business, especially during times of change.

Take a look around at the changing business landscape. High performance is no longer an option for companies that now compete in international or expanded regional markets, whether they want to or not. Technology-driven change is extremely rapid and is creating unprecedented competitive pressures for survival. Downsizing, mergers, re-engineering, and constantly changing customer demands contribute to the compelling economic reality that organizations must do more with less. Even as economic and business cycles begin to change and shift into growth and expansion, the competitive pressure is unrelenting. Organizations and individuals still feel the pressure to perform at higher and higher levels.

Stress levels for employees are extremely high, as they try to maintain balance between their personal lives and work demands. Many of us long for the "good old days," but are haunted by the creeping knowledge that the "good old days" are not coming back. These are the new "good old days." We had better learn how to perform, survive, and lead fulfilled lives in these challenging times.

How do modern organizations respond to these pressures for higher and higher levels of performance with employees that are growing more tired by the day?

## Enter Coaching

Progressive leaders are choosing coaching as a fundamental part of their response. Coaching is a healthy, positive, and enabling process that develops the capacity of people to solve today's business problems.

The premise of this book is simple:

*A performance-based, feedback-rich organization that is supported by coaching as a predominant cultural practice creates a sustainable competitive advantage over its competitors.*

Therefore, it is important that we take another look at this uncommon management practice and see it with new eyes—as a transformational leadership skill and a requisite for creating true high performance.

Transformational Coaching is the leadership process for the new millennium. It is a potent communication process that helps people connect to the performance of the team and to the things that are important in their lives.

Touching people's spirits and rekindling what deeply matters to them is what *The Heart of Coaching* is all about. We do not need another book on managing people that shows us yet another technique on how to get them to do what we want them to do. People are crying out for *real* leadership from leaders who are open and vulnerable and real. That is what Transformational Coaches learn to do.

## Trust Your Experience

*Believe nothing* that you read in this book. Rather, trust your own experience to validate the ideas and principles of human interaction offered here. If you chose to incorporate any of the practices described, pay attention to how your relationships are enriched and your results are enhanced.

The questions interspersed throughout the book are designed to stimulate your thinking and engage your heart. To the extent that you become clear about your thoughts, your beliefs, and your experiences, you will be better able to integrate coaching as a new way of thinking and a new way of interacting with people.

# PART ONE

# The Heart of the Transformational Coaching Process

THE TRANSFORMATIONAL COACHING process provides a useful framework to guide performance coaching discussions in ways that open up communications and build trust. It also creates a powerful commitment to mutual learning and a partnership for discovering the best next steps.

This part of the book discusses the business and human case for coaching, presents the Transformational Coaching methodology, and illustrates its application to enhance the performance of both individuals and teams.

### Our Deepest Fear

*Our deepest fear is not that we are inadequate.*
*Our deepest fear is that we are powerful beyond measure.*
*It is our Light, not our Darkness, that frightens most of us.*
*We ask ourselves, who am I to be brilliant, gorgeous, talented, fabulous?*
*Actually, who are you NOT to be?...*
*There is nothing enlightened about shrinking so that other people won't feel insecure around you...*
*As we let our own Light shine, we unconsciously give other people permission to do the same.*
*As we are liberated from our own fear, our presence automatically liberates others.*

**Marianne Williamson**

*To create a high-performance team, we must replace typical management activities like supervising, checking, monitoring, and controlling with new behaviors like coaching and communicating.*

**RAY SMITH**
CEO, Bell-Atlantic

# Why Coach?

*Implications of a Paradigm Shift*

In the past few years, an old term, coaching, has received renewed interest in business literature. One author after another urges managers and leaders to develop and apply the motivational skills of athletic coaches to their work teams. Business conditions today have made coaching an essential element of success. Let's take a look at the business conditions that are driving this change.

## The Business Case for Coaching

By now, most of us know that a *paradigm* is a mental model that describes a particular view of the world—a set of rules and regulations that define boundaries and provide a means for being successful within those boundaries.

A *paradigm shift* is a big change—a surprising, abrupt, unprecedented, revolutionary, rules-alerting change. When a business paradigm shifts, the success of the past becomes less relevant, because the criteria for success has been altered and a new standard established. The victories of the past no longer apply to the present or the future. The rules change, the roles change, and the required results change. Everyone goes back, however temporarily, to a lower point on the learning curve.

The business world is in the midst of just such a paradigm shift, as is shown below. The rules have changed. The processes that people previously used to achieve their objectives are no longer valid, and the traditional roles and hierarchical working relationships are no longer effective. High performance is no longer an *option;* it is a *requirement* for the survival of both individuals and organizations. Competition is worldwide and technological change brings new challenges on a daily basis. Leadership skills are needed now more than ever.

## The Changing Paradigm

| Dimension | From | To |
|---|---|---|
| The Competitive Environment | Local competition | Regional and global competition |
| Technological Change | Incremental | Relentless |
| Organizational Strategy | Growth through satisfying customers | Survival through meeting and exceeding expectations |
| Structure & Systems | Hierarchical with central authority | Networks with distributed authority |
| Culture | Turf protection<br>Conflict<br>Command and control | Shared purpose/goals<br>Collaboration<br>Empowerment |
| Leadership Roles | Manager:<br>• Boss<br>• Decision maker<br>• Supervisor<br>• Traffic cop<br>• Delegator | Leader:<br>• Coach<br>• Facilitator<br>• Servant<br>• Role model<br>• Visionary |
| Leadership's Core Skills | Telling<br>Directing<br>Controlling | Questioning<br>Influencing<br>Role modeling |

In this new world, the paradigm-shift question is: *What is impossible to do today (or is not done today) in your business that, if you could do it, would fundamentally change the way you do business?*

The answer is: *Transformational Coaching*. This chapter examines how and why this is so.

## Corporate Culture and Performance

Corporate culture sets the organizational context for human behavior. It creates the framework for performance expectations and the ways in which people relate to one another.

Authors John Kotter and James L. Heskett wrote *Corporate Culture and Performance* to explore the consequences of the paradigm shift for corporate culture.[1] Kotter describes three theories that link cultural characteristics with financial performance.

[1] The Free Press, a Division of Macmillan, Inc. (New York, 1992).

### THE STRONG CULTURE

Theory I hypothesizes that a "strong culture" will produce vitality and long-term financial performance.

*In a strong corporate culture, almost all managers share a set of relatively consistent values and methods of doing business. New employees adopt these values very quickly. The style and values…tend not to change much when a new CEO takes charge—their roots go deep.*
*(p. 15)*

Strong cultures are characterized by broad goal alignment (all employees marching to the same drummer), high motivational levels and the presence of structure and controls (but without a stifling bureaucracy). IBM is probably the most famous strong-culture company, with loyal and highly motivated employees. Wal-Mart, Procter & Gamble, and Time are also examples of strong-culture companies.

Contrary to the Theory I hypothesis, strong cultures are not guaranteed long-term financial vitality and high performance. Although Kotter and Heskett's data do suggest that strong culture correlates with long-term economic performance, the correlation is only modest.

### THE STRATEGICALLY APPROPRIATE CULTURE

Theory II holds that a "strategically appropriate" culture is the secret to long-term economic performance. Kotter and Heskett define a strategically appropriate culture as one in which

> ...values and behaviors are common, (and are) as important if not more important than its strength...a culture is good only if it "fits" its context...only those contextually or strategically appropriate cultures will be associated with excellent performance. The better the fit, the better the performance. (p. 28)

Kotter and Heskett say that, for example, "rapid decision making and no bureaucratic behavior" would be appropriate "in the highly competitive deal-making environment of a mergers acquisitions advisory firm." They cite Swissair as a good example of a strategically appropriate culture, as is the VF Corporation. The appeal of Theory II is obvious: it suggests that one uniform culture will not work for every company and that each culture must create its own strategy to meet the needs of the industry it serves. The culture must "fit" its business conditions.

But even a strategically appropriate culture is not immune to failure. Kotter and Heskett's study showed that, even in companies with a good fit between strategy and culture, change in the business environment (because of, for example, increased competition) produced deterioration in performance when the company's culture did not change. Companies that did well in the face of change, they said, "successfully adapted to change, despite having reasonably strong cultures."

Which leads us to Theory III.

### THE ADAPTIVE CULTURE

Theory III hypothesizes that the cultural characteristic most highly correlated with high performance is *adaptability*—the ability of the organization to continuously respond to changing markets and new competitive environments. "Only cultures that can help organizations anticipate and adapt to environmental change will be associated with superior performance over long periods of time," Kotter and Heskett say. They further define "adaptive culture" as one in which:

> ...*managers throughout the hierarchy...provide leadership to initiate change in strategies and tactics whenever necessary to satisfy the legitimate interests of not just stockholders, or customers, or employees, but all three.* (p. 46)

Digital Equipment, 3M, and Hewlett-Packard are good examples of adaptive companies. The following Performance Measure shows how important adaptability is to the bottom line.

**Performance Measure (over an eleven-year period)**

| | Organizations with Performance-Enhancing Cultures | Organizations Without Performance-Enhancing Cultures |
|---|---|---|
| Revenue Growth | 682% | 166% |
| Employment Growth | 282% | 36% |
| Stock-Price Growth | 901% | 74% |
| Net-Income Growth | 756% | 1% |

The Economics and Social Costs of Low-Performance Cultures (1977-1988), (Kotter & Heskett, 1992)

According to Kotter and Heskett, adaptive organizations tend to:

- Be run by strong leaders who are committed to winning the hearts and minds of people
- Give balanced attention to serving all three constituents of the organization: customers, employees, and stockholders
- Be highly energized and aligned on common goals
- Be receptive to change, responsive to opportunity, and dedicated to creative risk taking
- Provide a cheerleading, encouraging environment that builds confidence and morale
- Provide a high-trust environment that identifies and confronts problems

- Be filled with supportive and enthusiastic people who recognize initiative
- Emphasize fairness, integrity, and "doing the right thing"

It sounds like a great place to work, doesn't it? This almost perfectly describes a high-performance organization. As a matter of fact, progressive leadership recognizes that these characteristics as important to supporting high performance. My experience in large organizational change efforts, however, has shown that one element critical to creating these conditions is frequently missing from the equation.

The missing element is *coaching*.

## Mixed Messages

In 1979, *Training and Development Journal* published an article in which the following two figures appeared.

Figure A illustrates what seems to be a reasonable expectation of training: it will produce new behaviors that, over time (and in spite of a small and temporary dip in performance immediately after training), will lead to improved results.

Figure B shows what actually happens after training if no coaching is provided: old behaviors quickly resurface, and sustained performance improvements never materialize. Without coaching, the opportunity that training provides for permanently improving behavior—and for the improved results that could have followed—is lost.

By not providing coaching to people after providing them with behaviorally based skill training, we set them up to fail. Such approaches offer a mixed message; to the employee's face, we say:

*We will send you to this training program in which you will learn new skills and behaviors to apply on the job. We have selected you because we believe you can do a better job afterward and, of course, we expect to see improved performance after you return. Now, go and learn.*

## A. What *Should* Happen with a New Skill (with Coaching)

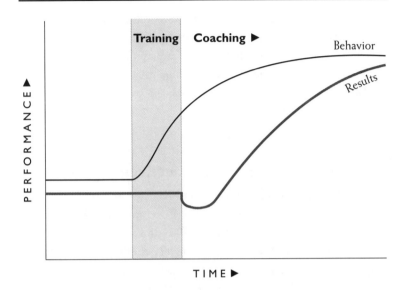

Adapted from *Training and Development Journal*, November, 1979.

## B. What *Actually* Happens with a New Skill (Without Coaching)

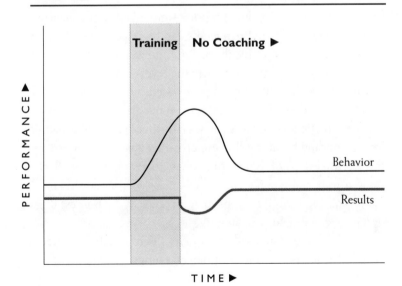

But the unspoken organizational truth the employees hear and usually experience is more like this:

*We hope you can implement all the changes we expect to see without any help from us, because we are just too busy to coach you or reinforce new skills after you return. But we know from experience that you probably won't be able to do it—the effect of training frequently is negligible. That's why it is the first thing we cut when times get tough. Thanks for going to the workshop!*

## Feedback and Leadership Effectiveness

A study led by Marshall Goldsmith of Keilty, Goldsmith & Company adds another dimension to developmental training and follow-up. It surveyed more than 8,000 "direct reports" about their perceptions of their managers' levels of effectiveness after participating in a leadership-development program. During the leadership-development process, each manager was asked to respond to direct reports who provided feedback to him or her, implement an improvement plan that responded to the feedback, and follow up with the direct reports as to progress made. Eighteen months later, direct reports were asked about their managers' current levels of effectiveness and to what degree the managers had responded to feedback and followed up.

The data were clear: the higher the level of response and follow-up, the higher the direct reports rated their bosses' effectiveness (see the following two tables for summaries of the data). Leadership effectiveness is dramatically affected through asking for, responding to, and following up on feedback, and those are the essential steps of Transformational Coaching. In table B, the trend toward more perceived effectiveness is pronounced and dramatic, shifting from 7 percent to 55 percent in the highest degree of improvement (the +3 category).

Let's take a look at another good reason to coach: the effect it has on the hearts and minds of human beings.

## A. Leadership Effectiveness and Feedback Follow-Up (Keilty, Goldsmith & Company, 1994)

| | Perception of Effectiveness As a Percentage | | |
|---|---|---|---|
| | **Worse** | **Same** | **Better** |
| No response/No follow-up | 19* | 34 | 48 |
| Response/No follow-up | 21* | 34 | 45 |
| Response/Little follow-up | 10 | 24 | 66 |
| Response/Some follow-up | 3 | 9 | 89 |
| Response/Frequent follow-up | 1 | 5 | 95 |
| Response/Consistent follow-up | 1 | 4 | 95 |

*Expectations were raised with responding and fell with no follow-up.*

## B. Detail of Shaded Area in A

| Degree of Follow-Up | Degree of Improvement in Relative Effectiveness | | | |
|---|---|---|---|---|
| | **%** | **+1** | **+2** | **+3** |
| "Some" | 89 | 44 | 38 | 7 |
| "Frequent" | 95 | 21 | 53 | 21 |
| "Consistent" | 95 | 9 | 31 | 55 |

# The Human Case for Coaching

The traditional approach to management has its roots in an auto-cratic, military-style "command-and-control" model that works well in the environment for which it was designed: war. But in most business settings, it has serious unintended consequences.

### Theories X, Y, and Z

Business researchers have described a number of management approaches over the decades. Two of the most famous are Theories X and Y, articulated by Douglas McGregor.[2]

[2] *The Human Side of Enterprise,* (New York, McGraw-Hill, 1960).

Theory X, a traditional style of management, assumes that people are lazy, uncreative, and need clear directions and penal-ties to support productivity. Two different metaphors are associat-ed with the Theory X explanation of motivation: the "carrot" (based on using *reward* as the motivator) and the "stick" (based on using *fear* as the motivator). The drawback with these two motiva-tors is that they are polar opposites and, therefore, provide no middle ground to guide a manager's actions in today's environ-ment.

*The carrot and stick are pervasive and persuasive motivators. But if you treat people like donkeys they'll perform like donkeys.*

**John Whitmore**

Nor do they bring out the best in people. The stick approach achieves compliance, at best. The carrot approach frequently leaves people feeling manipulated. We either threaten someone's job or throw money at the problem. Neither strategy works for very long.

One of the first essential things lost under Theory-X manage-ment is initiative. People learn to wait for "The Boss" to tell them what to do. In the worst situations, they degenerate into a state of "learned helplessness," allowing small problems to reach critical proportions because no one has given them orders. People learn to delegate up.

Employees managed by a Theory-X leader never develop a sense of ownership of problems. If The Boss makes all the deci-sions, these decisions never become the employee's solution. Consequently, people's sense of accountability and responsibility is lower than what is required for high performance.

Creativity suffers. Most autocratic bosses throttle their
employees' creativity by ignoring their ideas or ridiculing them
for getting "outside the box" or creatively interpreting the rules.
People treated this way become poorly motivated and ineffective
in creating innovative solutions.

When people are treated like cogs in a wheel—or worse, like
children—they are stripped of their dignity and feel diminished
in the process. Spirit sickens and dies. Unmotivated, emotionally
dead people never contribute their discretionary energy to their
work. They do the minimum they believe is required of them to
keep their jobs, then they go home.

Theory Y is a much more humanistic approach to working
with people. It presumes that people are creative, capable, and
internally motivated to achieve. The resulting management style
is more supportive and nurturing of people. This outlook forms
the philosophical basis for much of the material in this book.

The Z organization, typified by Japanese companies, takes the
long view toward building relationships and decision processes
that involve the collective whole. It works well for Japan, but
American workers are usually too individualistic to be able to buy
in to this approach.

## A New Theory

We need a new theory. Perhaps we could call it "Theory C,"
for "coaching." This theory builds on the best of Theories X, Y,
and Z and is supported by the results of research conducted by
Glenn Tobe & Associates. In this survey, managers and employees
were asked to rank a list of ten performance motivators. What
managers thought employees wanted most from their jobs and
what employees said they wanted most bore little resemblance
to each other. Here are the results:

| Managers | Employees |
|----------|-----------|
| 1. Good wages | 1. Appreciation |
| 2. Job security | 2. Feeling "in" on things |
| 3. Promotion opportunities | 3. Understanding attitude |
| 4. Good working conditions | 4. Job security |
| 5. Interesting work | 5. Good wages |
| 6. Loyalty from management | 6. Interesting work |
| 7. Tactful discipline | 7. Promotion opportunities |
| 8. Appreciation | 8. Loyalty from management |
| 9. Understanding attitude | 9. Good working conditions |
| 10. Feeling "in" on things | 10. Tactful discipline |

The three top motivators on the employees' list—appreciation, feeling "in" on things, and an understanding attitude—landed in the bottom three positions on the managers' list. Managers' assumptions of the top three only made the middle of the employees' list. Many managers, however, still operate on these erroneous assumptions—with disappointing results.

Theory C would hypothesize that people are motivated by:

- The intrinsic satisfaction of accomplishing the work itself

- Emotional ownership of the work, which occurs when they are allowed to be creative (and creativity can be nurtured in anyone)

- The opportunity to understand and contribute to goals that are meaningful to the organization

- Leaders and managers who provide *direction* (vision) rather than *directions*, who are honest yet compassionate in all their communications, and who challenge and support people in achieving their goals

- Feeling appreciated and knowing that they matter to the company they work for and the people they work with

This is a theory of empowerment and it is the foundation for everything in *The Heart of Coaching*. The four management theories are compared below.

## Comparison of Management Theories

| Attitude Toward | Theory X | Theory Y | The Z Organization | Theory C: Transformational Coaching |
|---|---|---|---|---|
| Work | Is essentially distasteful | Is natural, at least under favorable conditions | Is provided for a lifetime | Is one source of fulfillment and growth |
| Creativity | Workers have little capacity | Workers have much capacity | Subsumed by the collective ·wisdom | Creative choices unleash commitment and a sense of ownership |
| Motivation | People are irresponsible and lazy; they need a boss and orders to follow | People are internally motivated; motivation operates at social, self-esteem, and self-actualization levels | Belonging to the whole is the motivation. High social involvement; blending | Opportunity to contribute to meaningful goals; focus is on self-esteem and self-actualization |
| Management Approach | Highly structured and controlled; short-term fixes are the order of the day | Openness and trust; support and encouragement | Consensus decision-making; slow process; holistic concern | People are treated as adults, with honesty; vision is provided for direction; coaches challenge and support performance |

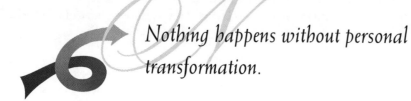

*Nothing happens without personal transformation.*

W. EDWARDS DEMING

# Transformational Coaching Defined

## What It Is and Its Connection to Leadership

Transformational Coaching is:

*a comprehensive communication process in which the coach provides performance feedback to the coachee. Topics include broad, work-related dimensions of performance (personal, interpersonal, or technical) that affect the coachee's ability and willingness to contribute to meaningful personal and organizational goals.*

*The Transformational Coach's intention is to help people enhance their effectiveness. The coach does this by delivering performance feedback respectfully, with permission, and in a way that the coachee finds helpful.*

*The process is transformational because it creates egalitarian, mutually supportive partnerships between people that transcend the traditional boss/subordinate relationship.*

Further, it is a broad, performance-management practice sufficiently comprehensive to include the entire range of helpful management behavior toward employees. Coaches help people clarify and reconnect to their purposes, values, and roles. A coach acts as a guide by challenging and supporting people in achieving their performance objectives.

## The Meaning of Transformation

Let's talk about what "transformation" is and why this process fits that description.

Transformation is huge, sweeping change. To transform means to change in the way that a caterpillar transforms into a butterfly, or a baby into a child, and then into an adult. After the process is completed, the older form ceases to exist. Ice no longer resembles water after its transformation; steam no longer has the properties of water.

The outcomes from applying the approach described in *The Heart of Coaching* are transformational as well. The process transforms the way that you, as coach, begin to think about this role. It transforms your actions. It transforms your relationships. With transformed thought and behavior on behalf of the coach, and transformed working relationships built on mutual trust and respect, the working results are transformed. Greater resiliency and trust in the relationship create a more resourceful, creative reservoir from which to draw business solutions for challenges faced by individuals and the enterprise.

Using a big word like "transformational" to describe this process has many benefits. It certainly signals change. It encourages the coach and the coachee to engage fully in personal and professional development to support the accomplishment of goals and objectives. It sets the expectation that something big is going to happen.

In Transformational Coaching, we learn to look at business success factors differently—more broadly. Rather than focusing only on the bottom-line financial results, a Transformational Coach appreciates and develops the people and the processes by which they achieve those results.

## Transformational Coaching and Other Leadership Roles

Transformational Coaching and leadership are inextricably linked; "coach" is one of the key roles a leader must play. Leadership is not restricted to the few people at the top and in charge of organizations. A broader definition of leadership is:

> *The constructive influencing of others in the achievement of organizational goals and objectives by providing direction, support, and a positive example through role modeling.*

In my work with leaders at all levels of organizations, I have synthesized a model that captures the essence of the transition from "manager" (the person at the top, performing the traditional role) to "leader" (an expansive, new-paradigm role). This model (described below) builds on what Peter Drucker has identified as core management competencies (planning, organizing, motivating, and controlling) by adding five roles that form the essence of contemporary business leadership: visionary, servant, coach, facilitator, and role model.[3]

*We lead by being human.
We do not lead by being
corporate, by being
professional or by being
institutional.*

**Paul Hawken**

[3] These concepts appear in current business literature but are uniquely combined in this model.

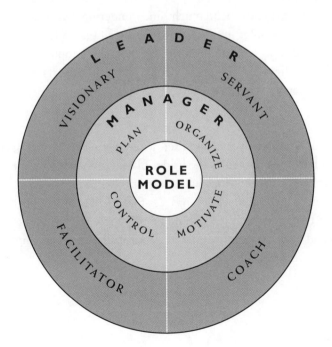

## Visionary

*If you can dream it,
you can do it.*
**Walt Disney**

Leaders must be visionaries. They must have a clear, bright, compelling vision to provide the people they lead with a sense of direction. Their vision sets the context for strategy, mission, and goals; it serves to lift people's expectations to the possibility of creating a more desirable future together. Even leaders who are not directly involved in creating the organization's vision can use it as a guidance system and a touchstone for themselves and the people they lead. Leaders continually connect themselves and others to the vision of the business.

## Servant

*I don't know what your
destiny will be, but one
thing I do know: The
ones among you who
will be really happy are
those who have sought
and found how to serve.*
**Albert Schweitzer**

The ability to be "in service" is a vital component of modern leadership. To become servants, leaders must mentally place themselves in that role, visualizing themselves in an upside-down organization in which the leaders serve others in the organization who, in turn, serve the customers. It is a huge mindset shift and is difficult to achieve. It is the rare leader who steps back and looks, listens, and appreciates the wonder of humanity surrounding him. Truly helping and being helped by others is an awesome experience, one we do not spend much time pondering. Making a real difference in people's lives is a privilege we all search for. Leaders are in a position to accomplish this by touching people in ways that honor them for the special people they truly are. The opportunity to serve others as a leader is a gift.

## Coach

*A manager's task is
simple—to get the job
done and grow his staff.
Time and cost pressures
limit the latter. Coaching
is one process which
accomplishes both.*
**John Whitmore**

Leaders can vastly increase their leverage by becoming coaches. Each of the other roles the leader plays is enhanced by the abilities he or she develops when learning to coach, because coaching is a communication process that focuses on connecting people to performance. Coaching helps people to clarify objectives and to discover more effective approaches for achieving those objectives.

### Facilitator

To "facilitate" means "to make easy." The purpose of facilitation is to draw people and their ideas out and to connect them (like an alchemist combines substances) with other people in a way that leads to positive outcomes. Leaders facilitate communication, change, collaboration, healing, connection, decision making, continuous improvement, and more. This list is incomplete but provides a sense of the initiatives, activities, and processes for which leaders need to assume a facilitative role. The paradigm-breaking portion of this role is to empower others to act on the organization's behalf by relinquishing control. This is easy to say and harder to accomplish.

> *When actions are performed without unnecessary speech, the people say, "We did it ourselves."*
> **Lao-Tsu**

### Role Model

The heart of leadership is to model the attitudes and behaviors valued by the organization. Those leaders at or near the top of organizations, by virtue of their highly visible positions, possess an incredible amount of influence over people's attitudes and behaviors. They define the culture by their words, actions, and deeds. They set the tone, pace, expectations, and standards for conduct across the organization. The shadows they cast are bigger than life, endure after they are gone, and constitute how they are remembered. In being role models, they create their legacies. Mid-level leaders, including first line supervisors, have the same ability to influence others by their actions.

> *Modeling may not only be the best way to teach; it may be the only way to teach.*
> **Albert Schweitzer**

## Training, Counseling, Confronting, Mentoring, and Transformational Coaching

What about other common management practices—training, counseling, confronting, and mentoring? Each of these management processes is a unique expression of coaching and occupies a place on the long continuum of Transformational Coaching. Although there are significant areas of overlap, and the terms are frequently used interchangeably, each practice has its own character. The most helpful distinctions may be in purpose, process, and content. Let's see how they relate.

### The Coaching Continuum

| Training | Counseling | Confronting | Mentoring |
|---|---|---|---|
| Technical & job skills | Personal problems | Negative attitudes | Career development |
| Policies & procedures | Personal-growth issues | Behavioral problems | Political orientation |
| Work-task orientation | Coping/healing strategies | Substandard performance | Networking & exposure |
| Goals & objectives | Physical & mental health | Persistent concerns | Cultural fit |

**Training** is the instructional process by which specific knowledge and skills are transferred to the trainee. Training usually focuses on technical job skills and orientation to the rules and regulations under which the trainee is expected to perform his or her role. Training is not optional, and usually occurs early in the employment cycle at any time when new skills are required. In a high-performance learning organization, training is an ongoing and never-ending process of continually improving the capacity and quality of the organization's biggest asset—its people.

**Counseling** is helping people who have personal or interpersonal issues, inside or outside of work, that are interfering with work performance. Often, this type of intervention leads to external professional counseling services, in which the focus is on clarifying the exact nature of the problems and healing the emotional issues. When counseling is needed, most organizations fulfill their sense of responsibility by finding a helpful way to see that these needs are addressed. Counseling usually is not optional, especially when management is aware of issues on which people need help.

**Confronting** is how we deal with negative or disruptive behavior or less-than-acceptable job performance. In this form of Transformational Coaching, the coach directly addresses issues and concerns about what is not working. The coach clarifies goals and objectives and the related shortfall of current performance, and then helps the coachee move toward solutions. When con-

frontation is handled effectively, it results in positive resolution
and changed (or enhanced) behavior and/or performance.
Confronting is not optional; it is required for teams and individuals who want to achieve high performance.

**Mentoring** is a process in which mature and more experienced
managers share their wisdom and experience with younger employees on a one-on-one basis. Mentoring typically addresses
issues of inculturation, career growth, political savvy, and personal
networking in the organization. It usually occurs within a formal,
structured program. Mentors assist their "mentees" to gain perspective, exposure, and opportunities within the organization.
Although highly desirable, mentoring is optional for both the
individual and the organization.

Because each of these practices can be viewed as a specific
expression of coaching, the Transformational Coaching model
you are about to see should provide a deeply helpful framework
to support your ongoing development in these related areas.

## Characteristics of the Transformational Coaching Process

As a practitioner of Transformational Coaching, I am always trying to learn and grow and become more effective. As I used and
studied a variety of coaching models, I became aware of their
strengths and limitations—especially the limitations of what I
regard as the "telling" approaches. In designing the Transformational Coaching model, I incorporated the best of what I have
seen, addressed problems inherent in some of the models, and
added my own ideas. As a result, the process of Transformational
Coaching is distinctive. Its characteristics include the following:

First, *it is data-based*. It is important that any coaching process
be based on objective facts; the coach shares perceptions of an
event or a situation in objective, behavioral terms. Although it is
impossible for anyone to filter out all of his or her subjective evaluations and judgments, it is essential to base a coaching session
on as objective a description of the situation as possible.

Second, *it is performance focused*. It is important to focus on behaviors in the context of the effect they have (or do not have) on individual and organizational performance. Organizations exist to provide products and services for their customers. Consistently achieving that objective extremely well is becoming more complex and difficult. Our ability to remain our customers' choice by providing those products and services at competitive prices is what this process facilitates. This model is designed to help keep the focus on addressing issues that either enhance or inhibit performance.

Third, *it is relationship focused*. As you may have noticed, the quality of people's working relationships form the context for their ability and willingness to work together effectively. Your effectiveness as a coach is directly proportional to the quality of your relationship with the coachee. Rapport, trust, and permission are the essential building blocks of an effective coaching relationship. Therefore, in this book you will find many communication processes that create a connection and mutual respect between people.

Fourth, *it is slower, not faster*. Most of us work at a breakneck pace. The unintended consequence of this fire-fighting mentality is often a diminished quality of interaction and communication between people. The Transformational Coaching process, when effectively used, requires people to slow down, listen more deeply, learn, and become less reactive. It requires more patience than most people are accustomed to exercising in their interpersonal communications. This allows them to become better connected. Personal connection is one of the missing elements in contemporary society and in many people's work lives.

Fifth, *it requires "dialogue."* Transformational Coaching is not based on telling. Assuming nothing, sharing feedback, asking questions, listening to answers, making suggestions, and exploring options are key Transformational Coaching skills. This usually means that a different kind of relationship is necessary. Information-age working relationships are becoming more egalitarian and less autocratic and include a mindset shift from being "The Boss" to being "The Coach." This will be discussed in more detail later.

Sixth, *it requires more heart.* I have been touched by the concept of *unconditional positive regard.*[4] This phrase defines "more heart." Being able to value and esteem people establishes a tone of openness, compassion, vulnerability, and humility on the part of the coach. Invariably, this improves the quality of the human connection and the coach's ability to work effectively with people.

[4] A phrase originated by pioneering psychologist Carl Rogers

Bringing more heart into work represents a dilemma for most managers in modern organizations. We have been conditioned to believe that the appropriate way to treat employees is to keep them at a distance. We think, *"Don't get too close to people. If you do, you can't retain your impartiality. They will take advantage of you."* We carry these messages around in our heads—what Peter Senge, in *The Fifth Discipline,* calls our "mental models"—and they prescribe how we are to act as managers.

Transformational Coaching is a very personal process; it will be neither helpful nor effective unless the coach is able to develop mutual positive regard with the coachee. Our humanity enables us to connect through the heart.

Seventh, *it requires humility.* I have worked with feedback and coaching models that assume that the coach's observations are always correct and the accompanying recommendations are always appropriate for the coachee, as if the coach sees all, understands all, and has all the coachee's answers. Nothing is further from the truth. Transformational Coaching is based on mutual dialogue, with the intentions of eliminating arrogance and fostering a mutual understanding between the parties. In this approach, learning occurs for *both* the coach and the coachee *throughout* the process.

Eighth, *it requires balance.* The intent of Transformational Coaching is to improve the balance in the thinking, language, and behavior of both the coach and the coachee. It aims to improve the balance between head and heart; performance and relationships; what is known and what is unknown; and mind, body, and spirit. To this end, legitimate areas for Transformational Coaching include not only the measurable results that management usually focuses on but also the subjective areas of attitude and behavior.

*Self-responsibility is the understanding of, and acceptance of, the fact that your interpretations, not outer circumstances, determine your ability to respond to people and situations.*

**Drs. David and Rebecca Grudermeyer, Sensible Self-Help**

Finally, *it requires self-responsibility.* People sometimes need encouragement to be fully accountable for the aspects of their behavior that affect others. An intentional and challenging thread of self-responsibility runs through Transformational Coaching. It is there to assist coaches and coachees to take conscious ownership of their thinking, feelings, and actions and the effect they have on their co-workers. A coach role models this value (among others) and explicitly uses assertive and self-responsible approaches to communicate clearly and effectively.

*Make your ego porous.*
*Will is of little importance, complaining is nothing, fame is nothing.*
*Openness, patience, receptivity, solitude is everything.*
**Rainer Maria Rilke**

*Coaching is a profession of love. You can't coach people unless you love them.*

**EDDIE ROBINSON**
Head Football Coach, Grambling University
(One of only four football coaches to win over 300 games)

# An Overview of the Transformational Coaching Process

This chapter gives you a job description of the coach and a bird's-eye view of the process.

## The Coach's Job Description

A job description for a coach would look something like this:
   The coach must:

- Understand people's roles and jobs at a deep enough level to be helpful

- Demonstrate or teach skills or approaches to the job

- Delegate effectively, not just "dump and run"

- Delegate important work to develop people and their capabilities

- Observe people's work closely enough to have relevant and substantive feedback

- Provide timely and specific feedback regarding what he or she sees and interprets as the results of people's work

- Support and encourage progress toward goals, rather than waiting for perfection
- Offer constructive suggestions and possibilities for change with the intent of enhancing performance
- Support concrete commitments for behavioral change, when necessary
- Empower people to contribute increasingly at higher levels of performance

This job description represents a compilation of thousands of people's input regarding what truly effective coaches do. The model that follows is a systematic and comprehensive framework that will help you meet all the requirements of the job description.

## The Three Phases of Transformational Coaching

Transformational Coaching is accomplished in three phases:

- **The Foundation Phase,** in which you create a relationship and the climate in which coaching can occur and in which you prepare for a particular coaching session;

- **The Learning Loop,** in which you share your feedback, listen to your coachee, engage in dialogue to learn from the exchange; and

- **The Forwarding-the-Action Phase,** in which you continue to build positive momentum and create a commitment for change.

   This chapter provides a brief overview of the process itself; Chapters 4, 5, and 6 describe each phase and step of the process in detail. In Chapters 7, 8, and 9 you will find specific guidance about what you might say during a coaching session and how you might say it.

**Phase I: The Foundation Phase**

Transformational Coaching requires a foundation of trust and shared expectations, laying important groundwork for what is to follow. The foundation phase consists of four steps:

- One: **Connect.** In this step, you establish the coaching relationship. It occurs in one or more meetings between you and your prospective coachee. Use this time to establish rapport, clarify your expectations of each other, review the Transformational Coaching process, and make a commitment to using the process in your work. It is also important to identify what job-related challenges each of you would like to address.

- Two: **Delegate.** After the ground rules and coaching roles have been established, the second step for coaching relationships between a supervisor and a direct report is effectively delegating tasks and responsibilities. In peer coaching relationships, this step is usually irrelevant because the areas for focus have been shared in step one. Peers could explore how each might support the other more effectively on shared work processes or special projects on which they directly interface.

- Three: **Observe.** Observe your coachee's performance, how he or she interacts with others, and your perceptions of results. Coaches need data on which to base their coaching. The challenge is to gather it with as little distortion as possible to set up the conditions for optimal learning.

- Four: **Prepare.** This is your internal and independent work as the coach. Become conscious of your thinking and the assumptions, interpretations, and judgments that may be influencing your perceptions. With this heightened awareness, collect your thoughts and develop the information and strategy for the coaching intervention. This self-awareness pays huge dividends in helping you to be objective and self-responsible in the exchange that follows.

The Foundation Phase is covered in detail in Chapter 4.

**Phase II: The Learning Loop**

This is central to the Transformational Coaching process. Its purpose is to create mutual learning, respect, and insight. Although the other two phases of Transformational Coaching are more or less linear, the Learning Loop is purposefully circular. Continue to iteratively use this part of the coaching process as long as needed to clarify communication and "get on the same wavelength." It consists of five steps:

- One: **State the Purpose and Request Permission.** Obtain permission from your coachee to provide coaching and establish the purpose of the coaching session.

- Two: **Offer Your Feedback** (the data) in objective, non-judgmental terms, and include your perception of the ROI (the result, outcome, or impact) that the behavior had on performance and personal working relationships. It is usually helpful to include your feelings in a self-responsible way, as this is also data that relates to the situation.

- Three: **Ask Questions and Listen.** Ask an effective question and really listen to the answer. Being fully present to your coachee and listening with your heart are simple yet profound ways to gain all the learning available from this step.

- Four: **Share Your Related Personal Experience.** If you have a personal experience that might be helpful for the coachee to hear, share what obstacles you faced, how you handled them, and what you learned about yourself in the process.

- Five: **Use Dialogue To Gain Insight.** Engage in a two-way, respectful flow of thoughts, ideas, and perceptions to learn about the other person's sense of reality. You are finished with this step when one or both of you have learned something (had an insight) about the other person and better understand his or her intent, motivation, and perception of the results.

The Feedback Loop is covered in detail in Chapter 5.

**Phase III: The Forwarding-the-Action Phase**

In this phase, the coach moves the action forward in several ways. How this occurs depends on the situation and who you are dealing with. Regardless of whether you are working with someone who is on the verge of being fired or a star employee who is meeting all expectations and then some, you will forward the action by some combination of the following five steps:

- One: **Reinforce Positives.** Describe what has been accomplished and appreciate your coachee for accomplishing it. Let him or her know that what he or she is doing is important, how he or she contributes, and that he or she makes a difference.

- Two: **Suggest Possibilities.** Check for permission if appropriate, and offer ideas and alternatives you believe are within the coachee's ability to control that might enhance effectiveness or help with a problem. If this form of coaching is ineffective, you may need to move into some version of steps three or four.

- Three: **Request a Specific Behavior.** Based on the recent performance of the coachee and the state of your relationship, you may need to escalate beyond offering suggestions and become more assertive by specifying the behavioral change you want or need to see. Being specific by explicitly stating your needs can clarify expectations for both parties and yield very satisfactory results.

- Four: **Require Behaviors and State Consequences.** If you have begun a formal progressive-discipline process, you need to state the behavior or performance required for continued employment. This communication, although still characterized as coaching, becomes directive in nature. It includes a timetable and full disclosure of the consequences of not meeting the requirements.

- Five: **Obtain Action Commitment and Offer Support.** When it might help the coachee gain focus and closure, request a clear commitment about what is going to happen

next and when. For the purpose of demonstrating support
and the spirit of partnership, the coach should offer support
to the coachee without taking ownership of any "problem"
that belongs to the coachee.

Chapter 6 covers the details of the Forwarding-the-Action
Phase.

If this third part of the process model seems familiar, it is.
Most managers and leaders have a bias to focus on Forwarding-
the-Action. "Make things happen NOW!" is classic Theory X in
action—driving, pushing, and demanding results. It is comfortable and familiar, yet this vital part of the coaching process often
leads to unproductive stress, resistance, and resentment on behalf
of all parties because little or no learning transpires to support
committed action. That is what the first two phases of the Transformational Coaching process are designed to create.

Let's look at them in more detail.

 *Relationship is surely the mirror in which you discover yourself.*

**KRISHNAMURTI**

# The Foundation Phase

*Connect, Delegate, Observe and Prepare*

This phase consists of four steps: connecting, delegating, observing, and preparing. These steps flow chronologically, each one building on the preceding and forming the basis for the next step.

## One: Connect

This is the time when the coach and the coachee establish the rapport and trust that create an enduring coaching relationship. In this first meeting, several topics should be discussed fully and explicitly. Coach and prospective coachee should use this time to:

- Get to know one another as people—share personal aspects of one another's lives that may be unknown, yet appropriate to know

- Develop a common understanding of the purpose and process of Transformational Coaching

- Establish expectations for the mutual coaching roles each will play

**Transformational Coaching: The Foundation Phase**

Connect

Delegate

Observe

Prepare

FOUNDATION

FORWARDING THE ACTION

LEARNING LOOP

- Make a commitment to using the Transformational Coaching process as they work together

- Discuss the goals or objectives that will be the initial focus of the coaching sessions

- Share how each wants to be coached in this two-way process.

## The Creation of Rapport

Establishing rapport is critical to the success of the coaching relationship. Here are several steps to guide your behavior through the ongoing process of developing rapport with people.

- Be approachable and easy to talk to; take the time to be available to listen

- Be a "safe" person who does not hold what people say against them and never engages in any kind of reprisal

- Acknowledge people when they speak; appreciate that their communication may involve personal risk taking

- Validate their experience through empathic and reflective listening

- Be open and authentic in sharing your thoughts and feelings and the lessons learned from your life experiences

- Build and nurture trust in all your relationships

- Find the common ground—the dreams that unite you and the goals that you share

- Keep all agreements; renegotiate quickly when you see that you can't keep your end of an agreement

- Be congruent in your thoughts, words, and deeds

## Two: Delegate

In the common business setting between a supervisor and a direct
report, coaching presupposes that you have some*thing* to coach
about—a task or project that you have handed off for completion. How you delegate lays the foundation for any coaching sessions that follow. Poor or ineffective delegation guarantees confusion, disappointment, and ultimate failure.

Clear direction and goals are more difficult to establish than
most people think. The coach and coachee should work on goal
setting together so that they share ownership. Goal setting is
more effective if you use the feedback principles discussed in the
next chapter to clarify expectations and desired outcomes. Make
sure your coachee leaves the goal-setting meeting in an empowered state of mind, feeling confident and fully supported by you.

The goal of effective delegation is to give the person to whom
you are delegating the greatest chance of succeeding. You are
more likely to achieve this outcome if you systematically address
all the dimensions of the task or project you are handing over,
including its purpose, its importance, the details of the work
itself, questions your coachee may have, what success will look
like, and how the results will be measured. Each of these dimensions is described in the paragraphs below.

### Purpose

Let people know the real "why" or intent of the tasks you are
assigning them. It provides a context against which performance
will be measured and provides the backdrop for the action. For
instance, it is less effective to tell Bill to "Get the truck loaded
now" than it is to tell him, "Let's load the truck now because we
have a new customer who is relying on this first, overnight ship-
ment to get his production line back up." More information is
more helpful. This also models inclusive language, which
acknowledges that you are both on the same team.

### Importance

A few words about the relative importance of the task or project helps people to understand your sense of value and urgency

about the job. Convey the necessary overall levels of quality, schedule completion date, and relative priority. For example, link the task to overall mission or strategy (if relevant) and indicate how it fits into the bigger picture. Seeing how their individual work directly connects to the larger organizational picture is usually a powerful motivator for people.

## The Details

Fully describe the nature of the project to be undertaken, including all the nuances and fine points. Share any personal experience that may help the coachee understand the work. Share your understanding of technical or organizational obstacles. Most important, tell the coachee about shortcuts and remedies that might help things go better.

## Questions

Answer all questions. Make sure that the desired outcome is crystal clear. Encourage the coachee to reflect back to you, in his or her own words, how he or she understands the job. Be sensitive to the relative level of expertise and commitment he or she possesses. You do not want to offend by talking down, but you need a clear, mutual understanding. Using effective questions (see Chapter 8) will help you accomplish this goal and enable you to model this important skill.

## Success

Define what successful goal achievement looks like. Do not leave it to your coachee's imagination or assumptions. What will the project look like, accomplish, and so on, when it is done to high-quality standards? Your role is to set clear expectations with the coachee so that when the job is completed, nobody is disappointed.

Again, go for mutual understanding. Paint a vivid picture to make clear the results you (and the organization) are expecting and then ask the coachee to paint his or her version of the picture. Make sure that they match.

### Measurements

"No surprises" is the goal, so be clear about how success will be measured. What, how, when, and by whom will quality measurements be taken? Coaches frequently miss this step because it takes time to think it through. Make it part of your ongoing dialogue and follow-up process. What precisely is measured can be a collaborative decision, with the entire team involved. And, of course, keep a record of the commitments established, to be referred to when the assessments are conducted or reviewed. This provides great opportunities for reinforcing progress and celebrating successes along the way.

## Three: Observe

*One thing I never want to be accused of is "not noticing."*
**Don Shula**

In this step, you pay attention to your coachee's performance and how he or she interacts with others. You may want to take notes of the results of your coachee's actions and your perception of the ROI.

Your primary objective is to create a balanced perspective by considering how the coachee's behavior or actions (or lack thereof) negatively and positively affect his or her work performance and working relationships. It is valid to consider the effect on people and working relationships, as most work is accomplished in groups or teams.

Several guidelines will help you to remain objective in your observation:

- Suspend judgment
- Assume innocence
- Identify your assumptions
- Become curious
- Embrace humility

Each of these guidelines is explained below.

## Suspend Judgment

Our minds are conditioned to make snap judgments of situations and people. We attribute motives instantly, usually without a clue about the other person's reality. This is frequently followed by a negative assessment about the way the person did something, because we are often focused on what is *not* there, instead of what *is* there. We compare it to how we would have done it, and usually the person loses in our evaluation. (This is discussed further later in the book.)

*One way to change people is to see them differently.*
**Barry Stevens**

Effective Transformational Coaches learn to monitor their thinking processes and the content of their thinking. If they find themselves having critical thoughts, they learn to recognize them for what they are and set them aside, knowing that these negative thoughts will work against their ability to coach effectively.

## Assume Innocence

Give the benefit of the doubt to the coachee. Ask yourself, "How many people do you think get up every morning with the intention of screwing up?" Most, like you and me, are doing the very best they know how with the ability and awareness they have at that moment. This conscious question about people's intentions sets up the awareness that part of your job is to help people become aware of things they might not see. That is different from blaming them for what they do not see or for not being aware.

## Identify Your Assumptions

We all know the joke about how to spell "assume" and have probably experienced the negative consequences of not checking our assumptions. Effective coaching requires you to bring to awareness and validate your implicit assumptions for the following reason: to minimize their affect on your thinking. Additionally, it makes it easier to present and validate them during the dialogue that follows.

### Become Curious

The older we become, the wiser we are—when we learn to acknowledge that we really don't know very much. Adopting an attitude of curiosity, especially in working with other complex human beings, is both healthy and effective. It helps us to suspend judgment, which facilitates the learning process.

### Embrace Humility

In the musical *Brigadoon*, there is a song entitled, "There, but for You, Go I." Although it is a love song, it also reminds me that we all face challenges in life. I try to remember how fortunate and blessed I am and that I can't take the full credit for my life situation. There are greater powers at work, I believe, in my life and in other's lives. I have found that becoming more humble helps me to transform my occasionally negative energy into compassion. Releasing judgment against others is part of the journey of becoming a Transformational Coach.

## Four: Prepare

*The will to win is important, but the will to prepare is vital.*
**Joe Paterno**

In those coaching situations that permit time to prepare, the preparation step offers an opportunity for the important and significant inner work of the coach. A Transformational Coach looks inside to the thoughts and feelings that color his or her judgment and, thereby, broadens the range of possible behaviors for the coaching intervention.

When coaching is delivered spontaneously or in-the-moment, the discipline of this step will help the coach to be authentic and appropriately responsive to the situation, as opposed to being reactive. The following guidelines help in this process.

### Center Yourself

Do what you need to do to become centered, calm, and collected before you coach. In most cases, you will be more effective if you have adjusted your mental and emotional state into being open, receptive, nonjudgmental, compassionate, and willing to learn. Feeling compelled to deliver the feedback at the moment of upset is the first clue that it is probably not the right time. It is a wonderful time, though, to hold up the mirror and take a closer look at why you are upset. What can you learn about yourself in this moment? Do you ever do what you perceive the coachee to have just done? Do you need others' input before you (over) react? Use the upset to learn about yourself. You'll be a better coach. (More on centering appears in Chapter 11.)

## Handle Your Anger

Although you may have a message that you feel strongly about, you can permanently harm the relationship if you vent your anger, upset, and judgment on the coachee. However, it is important for people to be authentic. Having anger is normal. During the coaching interaction, being genuine about how you feel about the outcome or the behavior under discussion is appropriate. So, tell people that you are angry or upset or at your wit's end. That's real.

For example, what does not work is:

*"Henry! You make me angry every time you screw up on these customer quotes. You don't have a brain in your head!"*

It would be more effective to authentically say something like:

*"Henry, these quotes have mistakes in them. It angers me when this happens. We have got to start doing more accurate work. We need to talk about this and fix the problem—permanently!"*

What is not helpful is to let out-of-control feelings cause an outburst of blaming, accusation, or threatening language. There are many ways to ventilate strong feelings. Write a "damn you" letter but do not send it. Hit a punching bag. Work out extra hard. Scream into a pillow. Talk to a friend who can stay calm and listen, and perhaps coach you on your options. Prior to the session, use what works for you. Find whatever form of help you need.

To the extent that you can bring yourself under control and come to the process in a learning mode with the clear intention of helping, you will be a more effective coach.

*Helping people better manage their upsetting feelings—anger, anxiety, depression, pessimism and loneliness—is a form of disease prevention.*

**Daniel Goleman**
***Emotional Intelligence***

## Be Conscious

This is a time to fully disengage your autopilot and consciously bring forward what the Buddhists call a "beginner's mind." Remember that you do not know the answers, the reasons, the rationale. Be ready to ask questions and listen with your heart. In the coaching dialogue that follows, your knee-jerk reaction may be your worst enemy. Purposefully set aside your conditioning and look at the situation through the eyes of your coachee. Marvel at his or her experience. Be as curious as you were when you first saw rain or snow or your newborn child. Be open, not righteous.

## Demonstrate Vulnerability

In our society, being vulnerable often means being exploited. This dynamic is certainly true in competitive athletics, politics, and the free-enterprise system. However, freely giving your openness can have a powerful effect on a close working relationship enhanced by trust. A coach can take the lead by sharing his or her personal learning experiences (that is, mistakes). This makes the coach a real person to the coachee. When a coach shares at this deeper level, rather than continuing the exhausting dance of "image maintenance," the relationship becomes safer for both to learn.

## Limit Your Words

It is easy to overwhelm people with too much information, too many ideas, or too many suggestions. You will be more effective as a coach if you can restrain yourself from telling the coachee everything you think he or she needs to know about the subject. Prepare your thoughts and say only what is required to convey your message. Less is more.

Never use the coaching session to deliver your version of the Sermon on the Mount. Moralizing is a sure-fire way to distance yourself from the coachee.

## Contemplate Your Questions

Learning is best facilitated by asking questions from your heart. Offer them openly, without setting up the coachee for embarrassment or backing the person into a corner. Ask questions with a genuine intent to discover the answer and gain insight. Such questions invite people into the process of sharing, growing, and being involved. In this way, the coach becomes a Socratic teacher.

## Distinguish Between Requirements and Preferences

It is a product of our conditioning to see something done by others, believe that it needs to be done differently, and assume that we know the right way to accomplish it. If coaches adopt this (possibly parental) view, they limit their ability to share a wider range of options, alternatives, and possibilities with their coachees.

Learn to appreciate your ideas for change as *preferences* (suggestions, options, alternatives, different approaches) rather than as hard-and-fast *requirements* (unless, of course, they really are requirements). Usually, people have good reasons for doing things the way they do and good ideas for implementing changes. Transformational Coaches take the time to find out and, in doing so, involve the coachee more effectively in the desired change.

## Reflective Questions To Use in Preparation for a Transformational Coaching Session

The following questions will guide you through the process of collecting your thoughts and preparing mentally and emotionally for a transformational coaching session.

1. What have your observed another do or not do (or heard from a third party) that you believe would help the coachee become more effective as a result of your sharing your perception? Is it within the coachee's personal control?

2. What do you perceive as the result/outcome/impact (ROI) of the coachee's behavior on performance and people?

3. What personal filters (assumptions, attributions, beliefs, stress level, personal needs, etc.) may be distorting your perceptions?

4. How do you feel about what you are perceiving (pleased, upset, irritated, angry, delighted, hopeful, depressed, etc.)?

5. What do you believe to be the coachee's level of awareness, openness, and willingness to address this attitude or behavior?

6. Is this a good time for you to have an authentic, fair, helpful coaching session? Is there a better time?

7. What is the broad focus of the coaching session (individual performance, working relationships, career development, cultural integration, etc.)?

8. What is your clear purpose for this session, and what would you like/need to accomplish as a result? Do you have any boundaries or specific requirements that must be met? Are there personal preferences you need to communicate?

9. What history (past experience, including agreements and current level of trust) do you have with the coachee that could be incorporated into how you approach this issue?

10. What is your best judgment of the optimal approach to use with this coachee about this topic?

11. Is this a matter that should be documented for disciplinary/legal reasons?

12. How does this situation mirror something of yourself back to you? What can your learn as a result?

❧

*When I do not know who I am, I serve you.*
*When I know who I am, I am you.*
**Indian proverb**

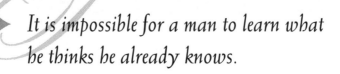

*It is impossible for a man to learn what he thinks he already knows.*

**EPICTETUS**

# The Learning Loop

*Dialogue Fuels the Learning Process*

The heart of the Transformational Coaching process is using feedback and dialogue to gain insight—before you launch into action. Culturally, it is normal to skip over this step because we are usually in such a hurry. After you read more about what is possible in the Learning Loop, I hope you are committed to making it a common practice in your personal coaching approach.

Let's start by taking a look at the concept of feedback.

## What Feedback Means

The term *feedback* originated in the field of cybernetics. It is derived from dynamics and issues regarding control. In closed-loop systems (such as a building thermostat that controls heating and cooling), feedback mechanisms deliver information about changes in physical states within the system, which allows the system to be controlled. Feedback is the data or information in the system regarding its performance.[5]

In a business context, feedback provides information from the environment about how individuals and groups are performing in

[5] For more background on feedback, read *What Did You Say? The Art of Giving and Receiving Feedback* by Charles N. Seashore, Edith W. Seashore, and Gerald M. Weinberg, (North Attleborough, MA, Douglas Charles Press, 1991).

## Transformational Coaching: The Learning Loop

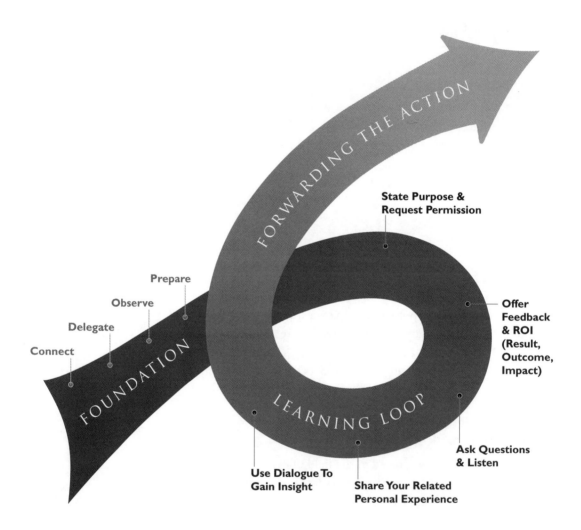

terms of their goals. Financial reports, performance appraisals, project evaluations, status reports, and a myriad of other tools provide feedback. In this context, feedback is also a *process* by which people share information and learn about certain aspects of work performance or the working relationship. However, negative feedback is not the same thing as criticism.

## Criticism

You have probably heard the phrase *constructive criticism*. If something is truly critical, how can it be constructive? "Constructive criticism" is an oxymoron; these two conditions can not coexist. The affect of criticism on human beings, regardless of intent, is almost always negative.

Whether you call it constructive or destructive, criticism does not work very well. People usually do not feel helped when they are being criticized. Criticism is usually:

- A personal attack
- Focused on the problem rather than the solution
- Destructive, rather than constructive (even when it is called "constructive")
- Focused on past instead of future performance

Most critics are difficult people to work with. Their energy is usually negative or cynical. They are difficult to be around, as they usually drag good energy down to their level. Their presence can make already challenging work impossible to enjoy—or even to tolerate. Critics typically stress what is missing or wrong with an idea. That behavior usually creates defensive reactions and a critical state of mind for the receiver of the criticism.

The most important and helpful energy to create and nurture in people is positive energy. Although you need to acknowledge the reality of the business situation, learn to stress the positives, the possibilities, and the potential for greater things. This focus stimulates openness, innovation, and creativity and is a more helpful framework for solving problems. Helping people to focus on the path forward is much more productive than keeping them hung up on what is wrong. (More on this appears in Chapter 6.)

*"Constructive Criticism" is a scam run by people who want to beat you up. And they want you to believe that they are doing it for your own good.*

**Cheri Huber**
***There Is Nothing Wrong With You***

Of course, some feedback is going to be negative. But the experience of receiving it does not have to be. When you have negative performance feedback to deliver, you will be more congruent with the intent and energy of coaching if you refer to it as *feedback, constructive feedback,* or *coaching.* Calling it *constructive criticism* sends a mixed message.

## Steps of the Learning Loop

With this background in feedback, let's look at the five steps of the Learning Loop:

- One: State the Purpose and Request Permission
- Two: Offer Your Feedback and Perception of the ROI
- Three: Ask Questions and Listen
- Four: Share Related Personal Experience
- Five: Use Dialogue To Gain Insight

## One: State the Purpose and Request Permission

It is helpful to explicitly disclose your purpose up front. Hearing your intent will tend to put the recipient of the feedback at ease. Some supervisors inadvertently send shivers up and down the spines of their direct reports when they say (or worse yet, have others pass on the message), "I want to see you in my office right now." Many people's minds go straight to "Uh oh! What have I done now?"

Requesting and receiving permission to give feedback is one of the most crucial steps in the Transformational Coaching process.

When you ask permission, you give your coachee an opportunity to make sure that it is a good time and the right place, that he or she can give you full attention, and that he or she is willing and able to listen. All these conditions must be in place for feedback to be heard. The simple act of asking permission demonstrates respect, which is the foundation for trust. You owe your coachee the opportunity to decline and wait for another time and place that will better meet his or her needs.

It is easy to catch people off-guard. If your coachee is under stress, in a low state of mind, or in a bad mood, a good coaching session is not likely to occur. In fact, you can damage trust by dumping feedback on someone whose plate is already full. Although it may seem extreme, I suggest that you *not proceed* with coaching unless you determine that the person is truly open to it right then. No permission, no coaching. It is better to defer it to another time.

There are, of course, situations (such as award ceremonies or company-wide celebrations) in which it is impractical to request permission to offer feedback, especially if it is positive. But even in an established, time-tested coaching relationship, it is best to check anyway.

Stating your purpose and asking for permission is simple and straightforward and sounds like this:

> *"Hey, Joe. I've got an idea that might help you on your project. Have you got a minute?"*

## Two: Offer Your Feedback and Perception of the ROI

In this step, you share with your coachee what you have observed and experienced and how you perceive its effect on performance and working relationships.

### Offer Your Feedback

Share the experience on which your feedback is based. Describe your personal experience as an observation. Be as objective and factual as possible; avoid assuming, blaming, accusing, criticizing, or judging. Remember to use self-responsible language. Begin your statements with the word "I."

Building on our conversation with Joe:

> *"I noticed yesterday in our meeting with Production that you seemed perturbed and upset. You responded with a little bit of an angry tone in your voice to Gene's questions. At least it seemed that way to me."*

*What gets measured,
gets done.
What gets measured and
fed back gets done well.
What gets rewarded
gets repeated.*
**John E. Jones**

Before we complete this running example with Joe, let's take an in-depth look at the important aspects of feedback that make it most "hearable" to the coachee.

## Qualities of Effective Feedback

Delivering feedback is a key skill of Transformational Coaching. It forms a foundation on which the coaching relationship is built. To be effective, feedback must:

- Be based on *direct observation*
- Be understood as a *subjective interpretation*
- Be *clear* and unambiguous
- *Describe*, not evaluate or judge
- Be *intended to help*, not to control or manipulate
- Be *delivered in the moment* (or soon after)
- Be focused on *creating mutual understanding* and dialogue
- Be *honest*
- Be *delivered respectfully*, out of care and concern
- *Presume innocence*
- Be *owned* by the giver

Above all, effective feedback allows the receiver to maintain a sense of dignity, self-respect, and control over his or her choices.

The following paragraphs describe each of these qualities in detail.

### FEEDBACK IS BEST IF BASED ON DIRECT OBSERVATION

*The simple act of paying positive attention to people has a great deal to do with productivity.*

**Thomas J. Peters and Robert H. Waterman, Jr.**

Pay attention to the behaviors and interactions about which you want to provide feedback. Feedback based on personal observation is possibly more focused and accurate. Do not collect feedback from third parties, assume it is accurate, and deliver it to the coachee as if it were The Truth. The human filtration process (described in Chapter 11) creates so much bias and distortion that you must be sure to treat secondhand feedback with great care. This leads us to the second quality of effective feedback.

## FEEDBACK MUST BE UNDERSTOOD AS A SUBJECTIVE INTERPRETATION

If you present information about what you have observed as The Truth, you run the risk of triggering a defensive reaction in the coachee. This, in turn, shuts down communication and learning—the qualities on which the coaching process thrives. When you use language that qualifies your feedback as *your point of view*, you level the playing field and remove judgment and arrogance from your dialogue.

## FEEDBACK MUST BE CLEAR AND UNAMBIGUOUS

Feedback that is crystal-clear and straightforward is most helpful. That means that you need to think clearly and prepare for the coaching session. (Spontaneous feedback is great, too, as long as it is clear and unambiguous.)

## FEEDBACK MUST DESCRIBE, NOT EVALUATE OR JUDGE

Feedback is most likely to be helpful and easy to hear when it consists of a simple, unadorned description of the behavior observed. Feedback draped in accusations, blame, or judgment is difficult to hear; the valuable information it may contain can go completely unnoticed.

Evaluative feedback sounds like this: *"Harry, you really screwed things up royally when you made those stupid mistakes. Why can't you ever get it right?"* Harry will not be able to do much with that type of feedback.

A nonevaluative, nonjudgmental version of the same feedback might be: *"Harry, I think I see a mistake here, and that is going to affect people's trust in these numbers. I would like to work with you on a way to keep these kinds of mistakes from occurring in the future. When can we talk about it?"*

## FEEDBACK MUST BE INTENDED TO HELP, NOT TO CONTROL OR MANIPULATE

Most of us have some control issues, and we all came to them quite honestly. It is normal (conditioned behavior) to try to persuade others to do what we want them to do. Controlling others is not right or wrong, but it is ineffective for creating high-performance, trustworthy relationships. It is a short-term strategy for achieving results, because people eventually see the manipulation for what it is and end up resenting the controller.

What is in question is the coach's *intention*. Foremost in the coach's mind should be the question, "What am I really trying to do here?" The true intention to serve and help others is far more noble than attempting to control them. Controlling is the predominant (unconscious) strategy of a manager locked into the paradigm of being The Boss.

### FEEDBACK MUST BE DELIVERED IN THE MOMENT (OR SOON AFTER)

The most helpful feedback is received very soon after the incident on which it is based. Stale feedback is almost worthless, having lost its context and relevance, especially feedback saved up for year-end performance reviews. Transformational Coaches need to create the type of relationships in which they can offer immediate feedback. The ideas in this book will help you to develop mutual coaching relationships that can support that level of trust and flow of feedback between people.

### FEEDBACK MUST BE FOCUSED ON CREATING MUTUAL UNDERSTANDING AND DIALOGUE

Mutual understanding is the overarching goal of effective communication. The Transformational Coaching process allows you to slow down communications initially, so they can be speeded up later. Mutual understanding creates respect, which creates trust, which creates appreciation, which creates dialogue, and so on.

### FEEDBACK MUST BE HONEST

In the Transformational Coaching process, coaches learn the value of accessing their hearts; in so doing, they bring more compassion into their coaching. Compassion does not mean "be soft on people." On the contrary, it means "be direct and forthright, yet respectful, in delivering the message that needs to be delivered." To shade the truth or shield people from hearing what you perceive as the effect of their behavior is doing them a great injustice. The greatest gift you can bring to your coachees is to be true to your innermost thoughts and deliver authentic messages honestly and directly.

### FEEDBACK MUST BE DELIVERED RESPECTFULLY, OUT OF CARE AND CONCERN

Caring is one of the basic reasons any of us chooses to become a coach. Coaching is a path of service and can only be traveled out of genuine concern for others. The essential respect we feel for others makes us humble and willing to drop our judgments so that we honor the contributions they make.

### FEEDBACK MUST PRESUME INNOCENCE

(These points build on the ideas presented under the Observation step in the Foundation Phase.) Give the coachee the benefit of the doubt. When you assume that another person is up to something devious or trying to get away with something, it affects your attitude and changes your tone of voice. Go into a coaching session assuming that the coachee was simply:

- unaware of how his or her actions came across
- distracted temporarily or under a lot of stress
- doing the best he or she was capable of doing at the time

Assume that your coachee was innocent of any negative intention to perform poorly. You will probably be right. Most people do not set out to make your day miserable; they set out to do the best they can, given the load they carry.

### FEEDBACK MUST BE "OWNED" BY THE GIVER

*Projection* is the process by which I judge you for behaving in a way—or for having a trait or shortcoming—that I consider wrong or stupid, while pretending that I am free of the same behavior, trait or shortcoming. A good coach becomes aware of this internal process and continually monitors his or her tendency to project. Transformational Coaches choose to work on themselves, especially when they become extremely upset or judgmental. They know that whatever upset them about the other person is also true about themselves—which is why they became so upset to begin with.

To "own" your feedback, deliver it in self-responsible language. This means using "I" messages. ("I am annoyed about your tardiness," as opposed to "You make me mad when you are late.") Remember that you can only provide information from a subjective point of view; you can not deliver The Truth. This is *your* truth, and it is worthy of being shared as potentially helpful information for another. This approach helps take the emotional charge off feedback, especially if it is negative.

*We don't see things the way they are; we see things the way we are.*

**The Talmud**

### Appropriate Feedback Topics

Performance feedback at work can and ought to be delivered for two main dimensions of performance: the subjective dimension (including difficult-to-measure attributes such as attitude, morale, and cooperation) and the objective dimension (measurable results such as sales, cost reductions and production levels).

It is important to deliver feedback for both dimensions because the subjective components make up the processes by which the objective components (measurable results) are achieved. Subjective components of performance include interpersonal and relationship matters such as:

- Attitude and morale
- Alignment with organizational values
- Alignment with behavioral expectations
- Communications, openness, rapport-building skills
- Coaching skills (giving and receiving)
- Leadership style and its effect on others
- Collaboration and teamwork
- Creativity and openness to change
- Flexibility and adaptability
- Personal attitude of accountability
- Honesty and integrity

The more objective components of performance include:

- Financial measurements of work tasks
- Organization of and approach to work

- Specific technical skills and competencies
- Specific behaviors and actions taken or not taken
- Achievement of departmental goals
- Sense of urgency, timeliness/tardiness
- Accuracy, thoroughness and completeness
- Planning effectiveness
- Persistence and dedication

### SHARING YOUR PERCEPTION OF THE ROI

Next, share your perception of the result, outcome, or impact (ROI) on performance and on working relationships related to the behavior you described. Bosses and managers rarely take the time (or believe that it is important) to share how the quality of relationships affects people's ability to perform collaborative tasks. Part of the Transformational Coach's unique perspective is a balanced attention to both task efficiency and relationship effectiveness. Make sure that you discuss whatever dimension you think has been affected.

From your experience in the production meeting, you might say to Joe:

*"I think your reaction had a negative effect on others in the room. The new supervisor, Ted, became a little irritated, too. The tone in the room changed, I thought, from one of cooperation to everybody trying to cover their bases."*

### SHARING FEELINGS

It is also important to include how you *feel* about the ROI. Bosses, believing that feelings have no place at work, often avoid or deny feeling content in work settings. Quite the opposite is true. High-performance teams freely exchange information about their feelings, both positive and negative, but they learn not to take it personally. In high-performance environments it is appropriate, normal, and healthy to share feelings, rather than to suppress them. Sharing them appropriately releases the emotional energy and passion that is a highly desirable commodity in the workplace. Transformational Coaches can be good role models of the appropriate expression of feelings.

In addition, the quality of interpersonal communications often is improved when people share explicitly what is happening at a feeling level. Offer this information in the spirit of full disclosure and authenticity. You are not likely to surprise anyone; most people are aware of your feelings anyway, no matter how hard you try to conceal them.

So, with Joe:

*"I feel uneasy that we may be getting off to a bad start with these guys. This new product line has got to come off without a hitch. This makes me anxious."*

### SHARING THIRD-PARTY INPUT

If the information you are sharing is from a third party, be sure to say so early in the dialogue. Better still, avoid using third-party input at all. Instead, encourage everyone to deliver feedback directly. When you deliver third-party feedback, you risk perpetuating an inappropriate (and usually ineffective) communication triangle, and triangles exacerbate problems more often than they resolve them.

As an aside, a productive use of a triangle would be to use the third party (with his or her permission) as a resource and coach for the particular problem you may be experiencing with your coachee. He or she may have helpful input.

After you have described your perceptions and experience, you are ready to start the dialogue rolling with a question.

## Three: Ask Questions and Listen

Ask a question specifically designed to elicit your coachee's response. Use open-ended questions that genuinely invite open sharing and begin with phrases such as:

- How does that affect…
- What did you notice about…
- What were your expectations when…

Phrasing questions this way invites coachees to share the ROIs that *they* perceive. Stay away from questions that can be answered "yes" or "no."

With our friend, Joe:

*"What do you think was going on with Harry and his team after things became tense?"*

After you have asked a sincere, authentic question, just listen. Demonstrate respect and do your part to build mutual trust by being sensitive, empathic, and respectful and by paying close attention.

Your tone and demeanor are critical to the learning that can occur in this step. Remember that you are sharing your point of view, not the world's Truth.

## Four: Share Your Related Personal Experience

Another important aspect of the Learning Loop is sharing your personal experience that could illustrate or connect to the coachee's current situation. Offer to share any relevant work experience that parallels the experience of your coachee and include what you faced as a challenge, how you saw your options, what course of action you chose, the results you achieved, and what you learned about yourself in the process. This creates rapport and connection and lets your coachee know that you are human.

With Joe:

*"I had a situation like this last year with...."*

Fill in the blanks of your experience and what you learned from it.

## Five: Use Dialogue To Gain Insight

Dialogue fuels the learning process. Given the daily demands of our contemporary work lives, stress often reaches unhealthy levels. In this environment, being patient with anything or anybody

*Authenticity in an adult is the ability to choose with whom and how to convey one's feelings, thoughts and boundaries in a self-responsible, non-defensive and respectful manner.*

**Drs. David and Rebecca Grudermeyer**
*Sensible Self-Help*

can be a real challenge. Patience is essential for many reasons. Dialogue causes us to consciously slow down so that more information can be absorbed. Transformational Coaches do not work slowly, but they know when it is important to shift into a lower gear and slow the RPMs of the mind to more effectively listen.

*Nothing is more terrible than activity without insight.*

**Thomas Carlyle**

This process of mutual dialogue and listening continues until the two of you discover common ground. Finding this sometimes illusive common ground means discovering the goals, objectives, or purpose that you share, making it possible to align your thinking and actions. It is easy to focus on how people and their opinions are wrong when they differ from ours, but that kind of attitude creates walls in relationships and maintains separateness and conflict. (See Chapter 8 for a fuller treatment of the art of dialogue and how to ask effective questions.)

In a coaching session, you can stop here or move on to the Forwarding-the-Action Phase (Chapter 6). In my experience, stopping here is not only possible but often advisable. This is because of the power of the Learning Loop. If the feedback and dialogue processes have been fully honored, the Learning Loop has worked its magic by creating insights for both people. Most people, when they have a chance to slow down and hear compassionately delivered feedback about how their actions and behaviors affect their teammates, are genuinely touched by the experience. When their hearts are in the right place, it is obvious to them what their next steps might be. It need not be stated.

As the dialogue process draws to a close, those who want or need to focus their actions will naturally move into the next phase. For these people, it flows effortlessly. For others, a gentle nudge is required. Transformational Coaches always invite people into the next step of Forwarding-the-Action.

&

*Imagination is more important than knowledge, for knowledge is limited
to all we now know and understand, while imagination embraces the
entire world, and all there will ever be to know and understand.*
**Albert Einstein**

*Learning is defined as a change in behavior. You haven't learned a thing until you take action and use it.*

**DON SHULA AND KEN BLANCHARD**
*Everyone's a Coach*

# The Forwarding-the-Action Phase

*Building the Momentum*

"Forwarding-the-Action" means making sure that the coachee's focus and momentum are great enough to move on to success. For a coachee who is doing well, Forwarding-the-Action can be as simple as showing appreciation. For coachees whose momentum is flagging, this is the time for firmer, more guided and assertive measures.

Remember the spinning top you played with as a child? People are just like that top. After you overcome inertia, they keep moving. But sooner or later, they wind down—unless you add more energy. Forwarding-the-Action is the phase in which the coach adds more energy.

Regardless of your coachee's level of performance, you will accomplish the intent of this phase in five steps:

- One: Reinforce Positives
- Two: Suggest Possibilities
- Three: Request a Specific Behavior
- Four: Require Behaviors and State Consequences
- Five: Obtain Action Commitment and Offer Support

## Transformational Coaching: The Forwarding-the-Action Phase

Obtain Action Commitment & Offer Support

Require Behaviors & State Consequences

Request Specific Behaviors

Suggest Possibilities

Reinforce Positives

FORWARDING THE ACTION

State Purpose &
Request Permission

Prepare

Observe

Delegate

Connect

FOUNDATION

LEARNING LOOP

Offer
Feedback
& ROI
(Result,
Outcome,
Impact)

Ask Questions
& Listen

Use Dialogue To
Gain Insight

Share Your Related
Personal Experience

Within these steps, you will choose an approach based on the current performance success (or lack thereof), the state of the coaching relationship (the level of rapport), and your sense of what would be helpful for the coachee at this moment.

## One: Reinforce Positives

One of the most powerful acts that coaches perform is letting people know that what they are doing is important and makes a difference. Ken Blanchard[6] says, "Catch people doing something right." If the ROI is positive on task performance or working relationships, acknowledge the good news. In American business, we frequently are so micro-focused on financial results that we miss tremendous opportunities to reinforce the positive and helpful things that people do to create those results.

[6] Co-author of *The One Minute Manager*, with Spencer Johnson, (Berkley Books, New York, 1981.)

As a Transformational Coach, you will not allow yourself to be tripped up by the following limiting beliefs that blind you to the importance of reinforcement.

- There is not enough time
- People just need to know when they make a mistake, not what they are doing right
- If you praise people too much, they will slack off
- People learn best by trial and error
- No news is good news
- It's not my job
- I might hurt his or her feelings
- I'll tell them when the job is "perfect"
- I wasn't coached and I made it

*I consider my ability to arouse enthusiasm among my greatest assets I possess. The way to develop the best that is in a man is by appreciation and encouragement.*
**Charles Schwab**

None of these beliefs will help you become a better coach. Reinforcement is easily and elegantly expressed just by saying,

*"That was a nice job you did yesterday morning with our production plan. I appreciate you professionalism. Keep up the good work."*

People value hearing these kinds of acknowledgments, in private or in public.

## Two: Suggest Possibilities

Check to make sure that you are still feeling connected and have rapport with the coachee. If you do, you may not need another permission check. However, if rapport has slipped away over the course of the conversation, it may be helpful to make sure the coachee is still able to hear (and you are still able to deliver) effective feedback.

A suggestion should be presented as something that *may* favorably affect future performance, not as a directive. Neither of you knows for sure, especially because the coachee will implement the idea creatively, as he or she understands it. It may or may not work well.

An open and trusting coaching relationship provides the forum for the exchange of lots of ideas regarding options, alternatives, and possibilities. It can be a great source of enjoyable learning, as long as nobody becomes too invested in having his or her way.

Possibilities for enhanced performance can be offered simply.

*"I've got an idea that may help you cut costs another five percent. I think you could be even more effective in reaching your goal by using a zero-based approach to next year's budget. What do you think?"*

A suggestion does not have to be a big deal. The coach is able to share ideas and the benefit of his or her experience in such as way as to be helpful. It is not a demand or a requirement; it is an offering.

## Three: Request a Specific Behavior

If the ROI is negative or there are aspects of the coachee's performance that you feel need to be improved, use a Behavioral Change Request (BCR)[7]. The BCR is a straightforward way to deal with a situation in which a behavior or attitude is ineffective or disruptive and is getting in the way of performance. It allows you to explicitly describe needs and expectations and gain a commitment for the behavioral change.

When this step is necessary, it assumes that the coach has already made suggestions but has yet to see a change in behavior

*I am always ready to learn, although I do not always like being taught.*

**Winston Churchill**

[7] A term learned from Mac Eaton, a heartful psychotherapist and friend in Del Mar, CA.

or an improvement in results. The reasons could be many: the coachee is just not trying, is not paying attention or is not focused, has a lack of rapport with or respect for the coach, or has any number of other problems.

If you decide to ask for a behavioral change, first have a clear idea of what behavior you want changed. Then make a specific request for the change and focus on being clear. Attempt to keep rapport with the coachee as much as possible, but be sure to be firm in your request.

A BCR might sound something like this:

*"Mary, we have talked previously about your being late to meetings. I noticed that you arrived about ten minutes late again today. Because this continues to be disruptive, I need to ask you to either stop coming in late or to find a replacement to represent your department. How would you like to handle this matter?"*

This approach reminds Mary that this has been an issue before and is grounded in recent facts. It is also nonblaming and non-threatening. The coach states a clear, rational need and holds Mary accountable to choose her course of action. The problem remains Mary's, not the coach's. What Mary actually does as a result of this conversation becomes the topic of ongoing coaching sessions.

## Four: Require Behaviors and State Consequences

If you are dealing with a problem employee, you may need to lay down the law in clear, unmistakable terms and fully document a progressive-discipline process. It may have become necessary to state explicitly the consequences of not meeting the requirement. Make sure that you are willing to enforce the consequences. Otherwise, you will lose credibility if you do not hold the coachee accountable for his or her personal behavioral choices. If the coaching process works as it should and can, it will be clear to you when you have done all that can be done to make it work for this employee. We sometimes lose sight of the fact that people make choices in the attitudes and behaviors they exhibit at work.

[8] Someone once told me that the term "firing" came from the seafaring days of old. Apparently, troublemakers at sea were tied over the end of a cannon and the cannon was fired. This solved the problem. With this image in your mind, maybe "releasing" people to other opportunities—where they have a better fit and may contribute up to their full potential—may become the way you prefer to describe this process. It is for me.

Transformational Coaches understand that the most compassionate act they may be able to perform is to release people to find other places to work in which they can bloom.[8] They have no regrets because they know in their hearts that they did what they could do.

## Five: Obtain Action Commitment and Offer Support

Regardless of which of the preceding steps you use in the Forwarding-the-Action Phase, it may be helpful to move to the commitment step because of the clarity it creates.

If the coachee has received your suggestion openly, simply ask what the coachee thinks the steps "going forward" might be. This can be expressed and acknowledged verbally or written down for additional clarity. Do whatever is appropriate and most helpful to the coachee.

If the coaching situation has already escalated somewhat, it may be more important to document the plan, using some form of performance contract that captures the commitment for the behavior or performance change and states the timetable. It does not have to be fancy but it should be taken seriously. Plan to follow up to ensure that the contract is fulfilled. Such opportunities can become turning points in relationships and careers. However, if performance fails to improve over time (with lots of ongoing coaching), the appropriate disciplinary steps should be taken to protect the interests of the individual, the department, and the organization.

Since the spirit of Transformational Coaching is creating a partnership, it is effective and helpful for the coach to offer support by simply asking, *"How can I support you in this process?"* Agree to those things that are within your control and are reasonable to do. If the coachee is under a lot of pressure to meet performance targets, the support will be greatly appreciated.

You want to avoid taking on accountability for what coachees need to hold themselves accountable for doing, but your willingness to support them sends a strong signal of true partnership and collaboration. That builds trust.

Examples of appropriate support include: touching base at certain times to offer emotional support and encouragement, reviewing work output prior to completion or presentation for the purpose of providing feedback, making a phone call to "facilitate" changes with others, etc. Whatever is appropriate for the situation and helpful to the coachee should be considered by the coach as part of the role of empowering the coachee to win.

Chapters 6, 7, and 8 clearly illustrate (with examples) the language and conversational flow of the process. It is really easy to implement once the purpose and intent are clear.

*I believe people will do their best, provided they are getting proper support.*
**Debbie Fields**

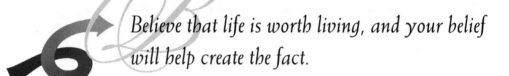

*Believe that life is worth living, and your belief will help create the fact.*

WILLIAM JAMES

# Coaching Language

*Finding the Best Words*

The words we use flavor everything we do. Coaches need to heighten their awareness and sensitivity to the words they use, becoming aware of the emotional energy and the impact they have on people. This chapter examines some of the more potent words and word combinations that, consciously or unconsciously, influence the quality of rapport and the connection we create and maintain.

In general, it may be appropriate to coach others when they seem to be unaware of how they sound. It is a coach's judgment call, but increasing another's awareness of how he or she may be perceived can really help the person to build rapport and trust with others. And, of course, relationships are the cornerstone of organizational performance.

## Specific Word Choices

A single word can change an attitude. The next paragraphs list word choices that can make a difference for you and your coachees.

### You vs. I or We

- *You* sets up potential judgment, blaming, and defensive reactions.
- *I* denotes self-responsibility and personal ownership of a point of view and is easier to listen to.
- *We* clearly includes others and stresses teamwork.

As you work to build collaborative and trusting work relationships, you will find that it is helpful to use inclusive language rather than words that separate or potentially trigger defensiveness. Self-responsible language always contains lots of *I's* and very few *you's*.

### Should vs. Could

- *Should* is controlling and over-directive and can set up feelings of guilt (which are not helpful).
- *Could* is more open and sets up additional possibilities in our thinking, acting, and cooperating.

*Shoulding* on others is an unconscious act of control and manipulation. Most of us do not appreciate this parental approach; in fact, most people are offended by it and resent being treated like children. Avoid *shoulding* on yourself and others. Good coaches have their antennae up regarding this particularly troublesome form of communication.

### But vs. And

- *But* tends to cancel out or discount what was said prior to the "but," and sets up an argumentative tone.
- *And* feels inclusive, makes room for other points of view, and indicates respect for the speaker.

Transformational Coaching is a process of sharing points of view that requires both parties to make a large enough "container" of their dialogue to hold all the ideas without anybody or anything being canceled out in the process. *And* does a great job of creating a feeling of openness and space for all of the paradoxes that coexist in life—especially in working situations, in which everyone has a portion of the whole truth and nobody can see it all.

### Try vs. Will

- *I'll try* can often give people an excuse for not succeeding, as in "Well, I tried."
- *I will* is a much stronger commitment.

Constructively challenging your coachees is part of the Transformational Coaching process. Stretching others begins between their ears, in how they think about themselves and their capabilities. A coach often sees more capacity than the coachee does. So be vigilant for "weasel" words that psychologically leave a back door open to failure. Encourage your coachee to make a commitment in the form of "I will."

## Jargon

Jargon can create confusion; it keeps some people from understanding and it sets up a sense of exclusivity. Common language is clearer and simpler, and it facilitates understanding by more people.

Most business environments develop shorthand communications over time. They are efficient and effective; they communicate a lot of information in a short period of time and are easier to say. Technical or industry-specific terms fall into this category. However, there is no substitute for full expression in common, ordinary words for the more subjective thoughts and feelings that arise during interactions at work.

Several years ago, I worked as a consultant in a large company that had developed a powerful set of shared values and guiding behaviors. The core values included specific behaviors that defined and exemplified each one. For example, the core value "integrity" had three or four behavioral statements, one of which was "speaking your personal truth with respect for others."

A senior leader in one of the divisions, an engineer by training, decided to simplify communications by developing alpha-numeric symbols for each of the values and its associated behaviors. He explained that, using his system, people could simply say, "Nice I-4, Charlie," thus streamlining the process of feedback and making it easy to bolster morale.

I had some concerns about the potential overuse of this shorthand. I shared them with the senior leader in two ways. I reinforced his commitment to consciously remind people of how their behavior was consistent with the values and guiding behaviors; that part was helpful to everybody and clearly was something that needed to be done. I then suggested to the leader and the team that a more effective way to accomplish their objective would be to better match the words of the coaching to the actual experience.

Instead of saying, "Nice I-4, Charlie," a coach might say, "Charlie, it helps me understand your thinking when you speak up directly and tell us exactly how you see it."

The leader and the team accepted my coaching—as far as I know.

## Body Language

Because a coach's first concern in communication is the quality of communication, it pays to notice how a message *lands*. Watch your coachee's body language and facial expression; lack of eye contact, folded arms, facial grimaces, bitten lips, and other cues can tell you a great deal about what is going on beneath the surface. The big dividends are in attending to and acknowledging these cues and helping people to work through the emotional aspects of hearing feedback or making personal changes.

## The Self-Fulfilling Prophecy

One of the key skills for coaches is reframing—helping others to think about issues and problems in new ways that help to create breakthroughs in their thinking and, thus, in their actions.

Transformational Coaches are sensitive to and aware of their personal thought and action patterns, and they help others to recognize their own.

Try reframing some common words and see what happens to your attitude:

- Reframe *always* or *never* as *sometimes* (hardly anything is always or never true)

- Reframe *can't* as *won't* (because the truth usually is *won't*)

- Reframe *mistakes* as *learnings* (because there is no shame in learning something)

And then try eliminating the following:

- *yes, but…* (because it is usually argumentative or just an excuse)

- *it* (because you can almost always more clearly identify whatever "it" is)

- *they* (because it separates and excludes people)

 *The deepest principle in human nature is the craving to be appreciated.*

WILLIAM JAMES

# Coaching Through Dialogue

## The Art of Conversation

Dialogue is critical to the success of Transformational Coaching. It is an effective approach to discovering commonality and connection. Using it takes discipline and a personal commitment to remaining open.

> *People are no longer primarily in opposition...rather they are participating in this pool of common meaning which is capable of constant development and change.... Thus far we have only begun to explore the possibilities of dialogue...but going further along these lines would open up the possibility of transforming not only the relationship between people, but even more, the very nature of consciousness in which these relationships arise.*
>
> **David Bohm**

## Why Dialogue?

The purpose of dialogue is to inquire and learn about others and to discover the shared meaning that makes human connection and aligned action possible. It is heuristic in that new information and perspectives emerge as the process unfolds.

Organizations are living human systems. Human beings have basic needs, some of which are fulfilled through their work.

### My Five Basic Needs

*I need to be seen.*
*I need to be heard.*
*I need to be respected.*
*I need to be safe.*
*I need to belong.*
*When all of my basic needs are met...then...*
*I'm ready to learn.*

**Anonymous**

For me, this says a lot. It is a beautiful reminder that we are all human beings and share fundamental needs. The implications for engaging in dialogue are tremendous. Sharing back and forth through dialogue is the process by which people connect.

*Dialogue* has its roots in the Greek *dia* and *logos*, which translates to "meaning flowing through." Dialogue can be defined as:

*The respectful, two-way, open-ended flow of communication that balances listening and speaking for the purpose of learning.*

Many organizations have cultures that inhibit people from really hooking up at an emotional level. I have worked with some of them. These organizations do not seem to have the spirit, the commitment, and the vitality that high-performing organizations possess.

Conversely, what is always true of high-performing organizations or teams is that their members have developed deep personal bonds with their teammates; these relationships form the context for achieving high performance.

Other terms of communication—discourse, debate, directing, and discussing—can be characterized as attempts to influence, impress, or control the other person. The best you can hope for in these situations is compliance, but more often they disintegrate into people becoming locked into positions and doing combat with their opponents.

# The Value and Power of Dialogue in Transformational Coaching

Dialogue creates a pathway and a safety zone for an open conversation in which both coach and coachee learn. Effective dialogue requires emotional safety for all participants; there must be no negative outcomes for expressing a point of view honestly and candidly.

Introducing dialogue into an organization (or a relationship) can lead to profound, positive changes in the nature of the working relationships. Openness, trust, willingness, and support are dramatically enhanced when open dialogue exists.

The conscious use of dialogue sends a clear signal that people are valued and respected as a vital part of the whole. It levels the playing field and creates a more egalitarian and participative environment. This is entirely consistent with the tone of respect and mutuality that high-performance teams create and sustain. Transformational Coaches lead the way.

The nature of true dialogue (as opposed to using words as a way of protecting yourself or your position) can be illustrated as follows.

## The Nature of True Dialogue

| Using Words to Protect | Using Dialogue to Learn |
| --- | --- |
| Listening to argue | Listening to understand |
| Pointing out faults | Clarifying with questions |
| Manipulating and controlling others | Respecting, valuing, and partnering with others |
| Proving one's "rightness" | Proving one's commitment to learning |
| Locking into positions | Truthfully sharing points of view and being willing to change them |
| Changing others | Supporting others |
| Protecting and defending | Disclosing and being open |

## Telling vs. Questioning

Telling tends to control conversation, shuts off the flow of ideas, and may trigger combativeness or other forms of self-protection. Questioning tends to open people up. It stimulates learning, creativity, and understanding. It allows people to own their own ideas from the beginning.

Recall the incident I described in Chapter 8, with the engineer who wanted to reduce positive feedback to statements such as, "Nice I-4, Charlie." I have reflected on that coaching moment many times since. At that time, I used the tool I had available to me: simply offering my suggestion in a respectful way. The response I remember from the leader and the team was polite listening and maybe a nod or two. My guess is that because the suggestion came from me, it remained my idea and may or may not have been implemented after the meeting. I believe I could have been more effective as a coach if I had taken a different approach.

If I had the Transformational Coaching model available to me, with its emphasis on dialogue, I could have helped the leader and the team start a dialogue about this very real and important aspect of changing their culture through reinforcing alignment with its core values. I might have been able to ask questions in a way that allowed them to discover for themselves the limitations of creating another head-based (as opposed to heart-based) communication system. If they had discovered and articulated that for themselves, it would have been more powerful than hearing it from me.

## Why Dialogue Is a Challenge

Western culture has conditioned most of us to use a telling style in our communications. Certainly, there are times and situations in which simply and directly telling somebody what you feel they need to know is appropriate. However, we often overuse this approach.

In the command-and-control paradigm, The Boss tells people what to do, when to do it, and how to do it. People who are bossed and managed in this way may never truly feel empowered to initiate action on their own. In these environments, risk taking is, sadly, an act of *personal* risk because of the organizational and political consequences of making a mistake or standing out by being different. One ends up standing alone.

Under these conditions, people's performance usually reflects compliance with the directions, rules, procedures, and bureaucratic requirements. Command-and-control styles that rely on "telling" techniques may create stability, predictability, and uniformity, but they do not bring about deeper commitment and creative problem solving.

Here is a better way: Learn to ask intelligent, effective questions. It requires a conscious effort to reprogram our autopilot responses by paying attention to our conditioned urge to tell and control others.

## What Makes Effective Questions Effective?

Effective questions are effective because they accomplish several things for both people:[9]

[9] Based on material in *Enlightened Leadership* by Ed Oakley and Doug Krug. (New York: Simon and Schuster, 1991).

- They demonstrate a willingness on the part of the questioner to listen for the answer

- They demonstrate respect for the individual

- They help people discover their own answers, rather than waiting for an expert (The Boss)

- They clarify direction, purpose, expectations, and goals, which are necessary conditions to create alignment across the team

- They solicit people's ideas, input, and recommendations, which creates a significantly higher level of participation and involvement

- They help people understand the roles they play in the problems that exist and in achieving improved results

- They teach people to contemplate their thinking processes

- They focus people's attention on the future, not on the past, and on discovering solutions, not on staying stuck in problems

To this end, effective questions must be:

- Open-ended rather than close-ended (they cannot be answered simply with "yes" or "no")

- Placed appropriately in the dialogue to clarify, illuminate, and draw out

- Authentic, coming from a sincere desire to learn

- Followed by (sometimes deafening) silence, to demonstrate the coach's sincere intention to listen

- Supportive in tone, to minimize the possibility of triggering people's defensive reactions[10]

[10] Tone of voice is extremely important. An unconsciously critical or intimidating tone of voice can cancel out all your good intentions and helpful content. Be sure to ask for feedback about your tone of voice, and take it seriously.

## Questioning Tips

Before you open your mouth to speak, it is helpful to take a moment to frame the purpose of the question you are about to ask. By sharing your intention up front, you set a context for the question rather than just dropping it on your coachee. People do not like surprises. It stands to reason that letting them know where you are coming from is really helpful to the process. It creates more openness to listen, effectively gets people's attention, and provides a clear context for the line of questioning that follows.

Ask open-ended questions rather than closed-ended questions for the obvious reason that closed-ended questions have the unintended consequence of shutting down communication. People respond to closed-ended questions with "yes" or "no" and that is not what you want. Open-ended questions require respondents to share their thinking and their ideas.

Phrase questions in such a way as to genuinely invite the other person to offer his or her personal response. Asking personal questions tends to force personal thought and expression. Try:

- "What do you think about this idea?"
- "What do you think is important?"
- "How would you solve this?"
- "If you were in my shoes, what would you do?"
- "What other factors should we be considering?"
- "In your opinion, why is this approach going to work?"
- "What do you see as the obstacles we face?"

It is helpful to have the questions begin at a general or higher level of inquiry and, through the course of the dialogue, become more specific. Here are some examples of questions that flow from global to specific.

## Sample Problem-Solving Questions

### Global
"How are things going?"
"What are your goals?"
"What are you trying to accomplish?"

*Never do for others what they can do for themselves.*

**The Iron Rule**

### Problem Identification
"What results have you achieved so far?"
"Where are you stuck?"
"What kinds of problems are you encountering?"

### Options & Solutions
"What solutions have you attempted?"
"What do you see as your options?"
"Do you want input from me?"

### Planning
"What is your "go forward" plan?"
"How can you apply what you've learned to your job?"
"Who else would benefit from knowing this?"

### Support
"What can I do to better support you?"
"Whose support do you need?"
"Would it be helpful to talk again?"

Avoid asking "*Why?*" *Why?* often triggers defensiveness. It frequently pushes people into a justifying or rationalizing mode, which is counterproductive. If you feel you need to ask "why," pay attention to the tone you use and be vigilant about the coachee's response, or substitute a phrase such as "What is it about that…" as in "What is it about that solution that made you choose it?" In the realm of feelings, rather than ask, "Why are you angry?," say "What is it about this situation that makes you angry?"

One of the most powerful aspects of supporting others with penetrating questions is that, if they are framed effectively, they empower people to think more deeply about their situations and, in so doing, to discover their own answers. The benefits include greater clarity in understanding, greater perspective, discovery of options and alternatives, and clarity about the next step. The coach functions as a guide and a sounding board who is proactive rather than reactive, which demonstrates a willingness to partner with the coachee in making progress toward goals.

## Transformational Coaching Used in Dialogue

Let's look at some examples to illustrate how the Transformational Coaching principles sound as they are wound into conversation.

Fred, the coach, has observed Sally, the coachee, make a presentation during a meeting. During the presentation, Sally did some things that Fred felt were less effective than they could have been. Assuming that mentioning those things during the meeting was inappropriate, Fred offered his feedback after the meeting was over.

**Fred:** *"Sally, that was a good presentation you just made to the marketing staff. I've got some ideas that you might incorporate for your next presentation next week. When would you have a few moments for me to share my thoughts with you?"*

**Sally:** *"Thanks, Fred. I'd like to hear your ideas and, based on my schedule for the rest of the day, I've got ten or fifteen minutes right now."*

**Fred:** *"Great! Let's go to your office and grab a cup of coffee on the way."*

In the office:

**Fred:** *"I saw you do a couple of things that I thought were really effective. First, the color in the graphics made the presentation very professional and interesting. It really held people's attention. Another thing that helped you make your points was how well you seem to have prepared this time. The effect you had on Jim [the marketing director] was clear to me. I think you've made him a real believer in the wisdom of this approach.*

*"Were you aware of the level of support Jim seemed to convey?"*

**Sally:** *"Thanks for sharing your perceptions of how you see Jim coming around to this idea. I was not as sure as you are that he was really getting on board. Obviously, I'm delighted that he is."*

**Fred:** *"Well, I really appreciate your dedication to heading up this project and taking the lead on these meetings. It's really helping us to establish our own credibility.*

*"I noticed one thing that you did in the presentation that was a little confusing to me. Could I offer you a suggestion on what would help me, and maybe others?"*

**Sally:** *"Sure."*

**Fred:** *"Somewhere I got lost in the transition between Phase II and Phase III. Perhaps some transition statement or overhead could be inserted there to better establish the linkage. What do you think of that idea?"*

**Sally:** *"I thought that was a little rough as well. Let me work on that this afternoon. I'll show you what I come up with before we make this presentation next week to operations."*

**Fred:** *"Great! Thanks again for a job well done. I'll see you tomorrow."*

Fred's intention was to be helpful and supportive and to reinforce the good work that Sally is doing. He also was able to offer a specific suggestion to enhance her effectiveness.

Let's look at another example—a situation that is a little more stressful and a relationship that is not running quite as smoothly as Fred and Sally's. In this scenario, George, the CEO, is coaching Peter, the CFO, about performance problems in the accounting area. For months, financial reports have contained errors that have caused tremendous problems for the company. This is another installment of an ongoing conversation between George and Peter about the problem. The first part of the conversation takes place in the CEO's staff meeting.

**George:** *"Peter, I know you've been working on the recurring problem with the financial reports. What's happened this last week?"*

**Peter:** *"I think we've got the turnover problem under control. Without John creating the problems for us that he did in his role, we should be able to attract and keep good people who are more qualified for their jobs."*

**George:** *"That sounds like you're going in the right direction. Rather than deal with the details here, let's meet after this meeting, okay?"*

Later:

**George:** *"I'd like to spend some time on this issue because it's critical for a lot of people. I think it's important that we talk about the underlying issues that, in my opinion, have contributed to the situation. I'd like to talk about your leadership, Peter. Is now a good time?"*

**Peter:** *"George, I know this is important. I want to learn from this experience and my guess is that you have some insights that will help me to be more effective. So, let's go."*

**George:** *"What I see in your department are performance issues that have occurred consistently over the last couple of years. I believe that you, as CFO, are having a difficult time confronting people* directly. It's great to have somebody on the leadership team who is easy going and fun to be around, but the implications for overusing that style translate to ineffective leadership.

"It's upsetting to me, and I think the division presidents do not have accurate, reliable financial reports. This year is tough enough without having to second-guess what the numbers mean.

"Are you aware of this tendency to smooth over performance issues like these?"

**Peter:**   "This is a difficult conversation for me, George. I realize that I'm letting the team down and I know these issues are affecting everybody. If I'm real honest with myself, I have to admit that I have a very difficult time giving people bad news. I see things that I know need to change, or could be better, but I have a hard time finding the words, and sometimes the time, to talk about them."

**George:**   "I appreciate your honesty and I want to coach you through this. I have a suggestion regarding how you might have resolved the issue with John earlier. Is it okay if I share it with you?"

**Peter:**   "Absolutely. I'm not sure I know what I could have done."

**George:**   "Earlier in my career, I had a guy who reported to me when I was in Operations who kept making little mistakes that, by themselves, didn't seem to be too big of a deal. However, since these mistakes were visible to the other managers, he began to lose credibility with his peers. This sloppy work was reflecting poorly on the entire team and, quite frankly, setting a poor example for everybody who worked for him.

"I got some coaching from the CEO at the time that prompted me to act on what I knew needed to be done. I should have addressed the performance issues with Charlie sooner, maybe with a performance agreement. I ended up doing just that, but the CEO had to open my eyes first.

"I suggest that you consider using performance agreements with all of your direct reports that clearly spell out your expectations and standards for their performance. Even your good performers would find this valuable in setting direction. It

*sets you up to coach them more effectively on an ongoing basis
and provide the amount of performance feedback that people
really need to be successful. What do you think?"*

**Peter:** *"This is a great idea! It sounds like a good way to establish
coaching relationships and to clarify the goals and objectives
that all my direct reports should be focused on achieving. I
really want to thank you for taking the time to share this with
me. Thanks, Coach."*

This is an example of the coaching process effectively used
to confront difficult "people" issues in a way that sets people up to
win. It was filled with dialogue and even included the CEO letting the CFO know that he was upset. This approach encourages
people to be authentic and explicit in sharing their personal experiences, thoughts, feelings, and ideas. The conversation was very
candid, yet supportive.

⚬

*For the want of a nail, the shoe was lost.*
*For the want of a shoe, the horse was lost.*
*For the want of a horse, the rider was lost.*
*For the want of a rider, the battle was lost.*
*And all for the want of a nail.*

**Anonymous**

*For the want of feedback, residue accumulated.*
*Because residue built up, trust was lost.*
*For the want of trust, working together became difficult.*
*Because working together became tedious, decisions were avoided.*
*For the want of making decisions, the business failed.*
*And all for the want of feedback.*

**Thomas G. Crane**

*It's a funny thing about life; if you refuse to accept anything but the best, you very often get it.*

SOMERSET MAUGHAM

# Special Coaching Situations

*Practical Applications of Transformational Coaching*

It is all just theory until you begin to apply it. In this chapter, we look at specific situations and provide examples of dialogues for dealing with them.

## The Difficult Boss

*"Okay," you're thinking. "This sounds great. Coaching is a 'top to bottom' process that creates safety, cohesiveness, and good feelings between people. I like it, but it will never happen where I work. Coaching isn't even a blip on my boss' radar screen. He's from the old school. He runs the business by the numbers. He cares about the bottom line and nothing else—especially not touchy-feely programs that waste time."*

I have known plenty of bosses and I have some good news and some bad news for you. The good news is that "Bosses" (in the pejorative sense) are a dying breed and will be going the way of the dinosaur. No one knows exactly when this transformation will be complete, but the signs are all around. The bad news is that you will have to live with them for a while longer in many organizations.

In the meantime, coach your Boss.

That's right. *Coach* your *Boss*.

If you "assume innocence," you can give the benefit of the doubt to your Boss. After all, he (or she) is most likely unaware of how his actions, tone of voice, bruskness, rushing about, changing meetings at the last minute, and so on (you complete the list) affect you and possibly other members of the team.[11] Apply the principle of "we teach others how to treat us." Take responsibility for stating your needs. Honestly and compassionately confront The Boss. If you have been practicing with others for a while, you will have developed some level of proficiency and confidence. Prepare fully. Select a good time, state the purpose of the meeting, lay the groundwork in your opening remarks, and stay the course. Trust the Transformational Coaching process to guide you through what may be a very ticklish and sensitive conversation. Keep the Transformational Coaching process model handy. Take it one step at a time. Keep breathing. People can usually hear what you have to say if you say it from your heart and with good intentions. Trust yourself.

Refer to the payoffs for remaining The Boss in Chapter 10. With those in mind, do not set out to convince your boss by arguing that a coaching style is better than what he or she may be doing now. Demonstrate the truth. *Prove* that your coaching gets better results by documenting the results and business outcomes that Transformational Coaching actually creates. This information can become part of your conversation. When Bosses begin to see hard results through application and mastery of "soft" processes, they will begin to respect you and your new approach. It gets results!

[11] Be cautious about using third-party feedback.

## Coaching Peers

In today's flatter organizations, more interdependence is necessary for high performance to be created and sustained. Not only can you coach your peers, but it is necessary to create an organization-wide, feedback-rich culture. This is covered in detail in Part Three.

Prepare yourself as you would for any other coaching session, focusing on a specific situation or incident. The feedback most people want to deliver to their peers has to do with issues of cooperation, support, and collaboration. Set the date and time and create an agenda that focuses on learning how you could work together better. Even if the other person has no familiarity with Transformational Coaching, you can facilitate the meeting and keep the conversation on track. Trust the process and your heart to guide you into saying what is appropriate at the moment. If your heart is in the right place, you will connect and have the best chance of working things out. This is not necessarily easy, but it is important.

## Coaching Difficult Employees

Sometimes it seems that certain people just have a way of really getting under your skin. You probably have relationships at work that challenge you to remain composed, dignified, or even kind. Difficult people have a way of showing up in everybody's life from time to time. How do we coach the "uncoachable?"

Think of it this way: In some finite amount of time, this difficult person will need to choose to "get with the program," or he or she will be working someplace else. Nothing is forever. This ought to give you some sense of relief.

Then, prepare well for this more confrontive meeting. Setting a helpful tone will be challenging, because you may be carrying emotional residue and anger from all the things you have left unsaid.

Do not think of what you are doing as "managing." People do not like being managed. Besides, a manager tends to retain the problem as well as the responsibility for finding the solution.

Become the Transformational Coach instead. Coaching is actually easier, as it maintains the ownership of the problem where it belongs. Keep the discussion on the behavior or actions that are causing the problem and focus on the ROI that you see. Stay with the implications for you, the team, and the person. People sometimes need to hear clear and direct consequences that communicate, in no uncertain terms, precisely what will happen if their behavior or performance does not change.

This is when you need to use the more assertive aspects of the basic model. It is a good opportunity to use performance agreements—signed and dated documents that specify all the major points of your discussion. Let the difficult employee choose solutions and hold him or her fully accountable for the outcome. You can do no less, for the organization's integrity and yours is at stake. Offer support, but be firm and fair. The fact is that some people will bloom better if planted in different soil. Releasing them, if done compassionately, is a gift for both parties.

## Situations in Which Coaching Is Requested

If you are like most people, you have already helped others many times with problems and issues. You may not have known it, but in these situations, you were really coaching. You can consciously apply what you have learned about Transformational Coaching the next time someone asks you to be a resource, a sounding board, or a source of support, especially by asking effective questions, listening, using dialogue, and prompting your coachee to forward-the-action.

Explore things like the nature of the problem, the goal or objective in mind, what solutions have been tried so far, what have been the results, what worked, what did not work well, where the person is stuck, what or who the barriers are, and what the person sees as his or her next step. Last, explore how you might support the person in taking action. The questions from "Sample Problem-Solving Questions" on page 101 should help.

## Executive Coaching

There is a growing awareness of the power of coaching for executives. Executive coaching has become a hot topic. Indeed, an executive coaching industry is in the process of being formed to serve executives in their development as leaders. Executive coaching is not a fad. It will become a requirement in the tool chests of leaders who wish to develop the perspective and skills required to lead organizations in continually changing conditions.

The executive coach performs several functions for the leader:

- First, the coach helps the executive to gather and interpret performance feedback gathered from psychological profiling instruments and/or organizational feedback tools

- Second, the coach is a guide through the executive's own thinking processes, helping him or her discover what next steps to take toward his or her goals

- Third, with permission, the coach probes and challenges these thought processes to clarify and strengthen the executive's ideas

- Fourth, the coach acts as a conscience, supporting the executive in remaining accountable for his or her choices

- Fifth, the coach provides emotional support for the process of change and thereby bolsters the courage and resolve needed to initiate and sustain positive changes

- Finally, the coach assists the executive to connect his or her thoughts and actions and create a balance between personal and professional goals. The coach helps the executive take action on what is known or has just been discovered

The key skills the coach must bring to this intimate relationship are: listening from the heart, effective questioning, establishing high levels of rapport and trust, and coaching the executive to take action.

The tool usually used to enhance executive effectiveness is a leadership-development plan, which is completed by the leader. Leaders who pay attention to feedback and respond with positive changes in their thinking and behavior (remember the Leadership Effectiveness Study cited in Chapter 1) are shaped by this learning process, just as professional athletes are. The coach often makes the difference between success or failure.

# The Heart of the Transformational Coach

WITHOUT HEART, Transformational Coaching is just another management technique. In this section, I explain what makes Transformational Coaching unique among coaching methods and how to bring the most helpful gift you can give, yourself, into the coaching process.

*It is with the heart that one sees rightly;*
*what is essential is invisible to the eye.*

**Antoine de Saint-Exupéry**

*Your education has been a failure no matter how much it has done for your mind, if it has failed to open your heart.*

J. A. ROSENKRANZ

# Why Does a Coach Need Heart?

*Bringing Heart to Work*

Most managers have been conditioned in traditional Western organizations, in which they have adopted a hierarchical command-and-control mentality. Moving from this traditional mindset into Transformational Coaching requires us to do more than learn a few new management techniques. It requires us to *change the way we think*. It requires us to discover *what* we think—about our roles and the outcomes we attempt to achieve with people—and to transform both our thinking and behavior.

Why is it necessary to change at such a deep level? Shouldn't business stay out of the personal arena? Why *can't* you just learn some new methods and techniques and begin coaching?

The fact is, personal aspects of our lives do not stay out of the business arena. Everyone brings to work the entire array of his or her personality—thoughts, attitudes, behaviors, habits, needs, wants, fears, desires, roles, and conditioning. Transformational Coaching does not *bring* the personal into work situations. It simply acknowledges that the personal element is a part of work and provides a framework—the heart of the coach—for dealing effectively with the whole human being.

## Becoming a Boss

Be honest, now. If you have had authority over others, haven't you found it compelling? Didn't you at times feel powerful and strong?

It is easy to see how even well-intentioned managers can enjoy the power trip of being The Boss. Most of us possess at least some of the human shortcomings that make us prey to this mentality:

- Our egos become invested in the roles we play and in the trappings of our authority

- We believe that, because we have paid our dues, it is fair to expect others to do the same

- We fear change and letting go of control

- We fear failing in the eyes of the world

- We develop habits of behaving and thinking that reinforce the "correctness" of the "Boss" approach

Add to this list the fact that most of our role models at work are Bosses and that the human system of which we are a part does not accept changes to long-established roles very easily, and there you have it: a Boss in the making.

## Beliefs and the Results Cycle

*The Results Cycle*, on the next page, illustrates the inevitability of this mindset. The key to stopping the cycle is understanding it. Let's begin with beliefs.

Our beliefs have a great influence over the ways in which we interact with people. As you can see in from the figure, what you believe tends to determine how you behave toward others. Your behavior tends to influence the quality of the relationships you have with others, which affects *their* behavior. This, of course, influences the results you obtain from these people. In turn, the results usually reinforce your belief in the correctness of your beliefs.

## The Results Cycle

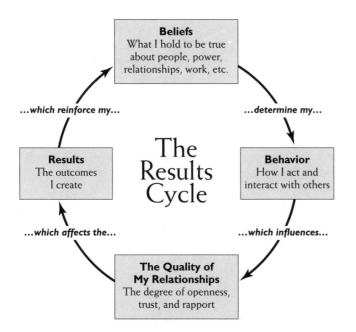

For example, if you believe that it is inappropriate to share your feelings with your co-workers, you might behave in very formal and rigid ways with them to keep distance between them and your feelings. If *that* behavior is experienced by some of your co-workers as aloofness or coldness, they may feel put off and intimidated and begin drawing their own (potentially negative) conclusions about your feelings. Because they do not feel comfortable communicating with you, they may do work based on inaccurate interpretations of your instructions rather than checking back to make sure that they understood. When you see the results, you may say to yourself, "See! If I can't trust them to get the most fundamental instructions right, how can I trust them with personal information? You just can't bring personal feelings into the workplace."

Another example: If you believe that a manager is supposed to be strict and unbending with the rules, you may be tough and punish those who break the rules. In turn, your direct reports may become guarded and stop taking risks. As a result, your department may do all right, but turnover may be high and other departments win awards from top management for innovative and creative solutions to business problems. In frustration, you may hold even more tightly to your belief in the need for control and adherence to the rules. This cycle is self-reinforcing and self-perpetuating.

On the other hand, if you believe that collaboration between people leads to better results, you might be open with your thoughts and encourage others to be open in sharing their needs and ideas for solutions. Relationships become more open and trusting; the people you lead are more willing to take risks with presenting ideas, and you get better results.

The easiest place to break the power of the Results Cycle is at the top, the beliefs. Which beliefs support Bossing and which ones support coaching? Here's a short list:

*At the heart of any good business is a chief executive officer with one.*

**Malcolm Forbes**

- Bosses believe that their job is to push people or drive them; coaches believe that they are there to lift and support people

- Bosses believe that they should talk at people by telling, directing and lecturing; coaches believe in engaging in dialogue with people by asking, requesting, and listening

- Bosses believe in controlling others through the decisions they make; coaches believe in facilitating others to make decisions and empowering them to implement their own decisions

- Bosses believe they know the answers; coaches believe they must seek the answers

*If you keep doing what you've always done, you'll keep getting what you've always gotten.*

**Anonymous**

- A Boss triggers insecurity through administering a healthy dose of fear as an effective way to achieve compliance; a coach believes in using purpose to inspire commitment and stimulate creativity

- Bosses believe that their job is to point out errors; coaches believe that their job is to celebrate learning

- A Boss believes in solving problems and making decisions; a coach believes in facilitating others to solve problems and make decisions

- A Boss believes in delegating responsibility; a coach believes in modeling accountability

- Bosses believe in creating structure and procedures for people to follow; coaches believe in creating a vision and promoting flexibility through values as guidelines for behavior

- A Boss believes in doing things right; a coach believes in doing the right things

- Bosses believe that their power lies in their knowledge; coaches believe that their power lies in their vulnerability

- A Boss believes in focusing on the bottom line; a coach believes in focusing on the process that creates the bottom-line result

## A Summary of Comparative Mindsets

| Boss | Coach |
| --- | --- |
| Pushes / Drives | Lifts / Supports |
| Tells / Directs / Lectures | Asks / Requests / Listens |
| Talks at people | Engages in dialogue with people |
| Controls through decisions | Facilitates by empowering |
| Knows the answer | Seeks the answer |
| Triggers insecurity using fear to achieve compliance | Stimulates creativity using purpose to inspire commitment |
| Points to errors | Celebrates learning |
| Problem solver / Decision maker | Collaborator / Facilitator |
| Delegates responsibility | Models accountability |
| Creates structure and procedures | Creates vision and flexibility |
| Does things right | Does the right things |
| Knowledge is power | Vulnerability is power |
| Focused on the bottom line | Focused on process that creates the bottom-line results |

# The Challenge of Change

If we did not get something out of the roles we play, change
would be easy. Traditional working roles and relationships do
offer a lot that is appealing. Let's take a look at the payoffs—and
the penalties—for not changing.

### Payoffs and Penalties for Bosses and Subordinates

Remaining a Boss has its advantages. For example, Bosses feel
that they are in control; are "right" a lot (at least in terms their
egos understand); maintain power, position, and authority and
therefore fit in with the establishment; make efficient short-term
use of their time; maintain old habits; and keep all their current
thinking or beliefs.

But they pay for keeping their positions as Bosses (rather than
transcending the role to become Coaches). The costs include losing the optimal contribution of other people's creativity; missing
others' ideas, options, and alternatives; maintaining ownership of
problems; and not learning from and about others. Bosses are
more likely to create resentment with employees. Furthermore,
there is always the risk that they will have the *wrong* answer sometimes (and create more resentment when they can not admit it).

There are prices and payoffs for being Subordinate to a Boss,
too. On the plus side, Subordinates have it easy—they usually
wait for The Boss to make decisions. They do not have to think
or assume responsibility, do not have to be afraid of making
waves, are safer politically, and can get out of many difficult situations simply by saying, "It's not my job." They are likely to be
able to retire on the job.

On the flip side, Subordinates must often put up with not
being allowed to think (yes, this appeared in the list of advantages, too!); not feeling valued or trusted; and feeling discounted
and diminished. They often have to deal with their own resentment toward their Bosses and they usually can not expect much
in the way of growth and development on the job. Their self-
esteem can suffer.

## Payoffs and Penalties for Coaches and Coachees

Changing to a coach-coachee relationship is not necessarily a bed of roses, however. It, too, carries compelling prices and payoffs. For example, coaches learn more about others and themselves, witness the development of other people's capacities, and build better teams. They also benefit from improved working relationships and performance overall and watch themselves grow and improve as coaches.

But they also usually find that the risks are higher (both personally and politically). They must learn to trust others more. Transformational Coaching takes more time and more personal courage than bossing. Coaches must share accountability. Coaches must become comfortable with confrontation of performance issues and they must let go of their illusion of control.

Coachees also discover a set of positives and negatives when they make the transition. Although they have the opportunity for more growth and development, being a coachee means that more is required than before. Their working relationships improve, but they have more responsibility and accountability. There is usually a new pride of accomplishment, but it is uncomfortable becoming used to new ways. They feel valued, but find that the new paradigm requires that they risk more. Work is more fulfilling, but they have to change. They are performing at higher levels than before, but it is not always easy to hear their coach's feedback; sometimes they take it personally by interpreting the suggestions as if they were personal criticisms.

If you look closely, you will notice some trends here. Most of the payoffs for the Boss and Subordinate are short term. The traditional Boss/Subordinate roles allow people to remain in their personal comfort zones.

The prices paid, however, are long term and weaken the overall capability of the individual, the team, and the organization.

This transformation is not easy. Each of us tends to be governed by our belief system about how things "ought to be." These beliefs filter our incoming experience, causing us to ignore what lies outside our own system.

## Beliefs That Block Transformational Coaching

It can be extremely helpful to acknowledge your own personal barriers. Do you see yourself in any of the statements below?

- "I don't know how to coach. I don't want to coach. I don't consider myself coaching material."

- "Coaching is not valued around here. There are no coaching role models here. I'll look different if I'm the only one doing it. I won't be supported."

- "The benefits are unclear to me. Look at me—I didn't have coaching and I'm successful. I'm doing okay; I don't need feedback."

- "It's not my job. Somebody else will do it."

- "It takes too long to learn to coach and then to do it. My immediate needs are greater than their developmental needs. Other things are more important. I'll do it later."

- "It is inconvenient. It's difficult. It's time-consuming. It's unnecessary."

- "Change is scary. I'm afraid to ask how. I'll lose control. I'll make mistakes."

- "I had a bad personal experience with coaching. It doesn't really work."

- "I don't trust others to coach me. I do not want to confront others."

- "I can't change. I don't want to change."

- "It won't make a difference. People won't change with coaching. People won't keep their agreements. People don't want to be coached. People are really lazy and won't respond. My people already know what I think about them."

- "It's just another management fad. Coaching is just a fancy word for 'bossing' people around."

- "Real work is more important."

Looking at the above list, which ones might describe beliefs you can identify as your own? Are they close? Are there other beliefs you may hold about coaching?

If you are committed to becoming a coach, these beliefs will act as anchors around your neck. Suspend them for a moment while we look at a belief system that may support your changing your personal Results Cycle as a Transformational Coach.

## Empowering Beliefs of a Coach

Just as Bosses have underlying belief systems that support their Results Cycle, coaches have beliefs that support theirs. Let's explore their thinking.

*As a supervisor, manager, or leader, I am responsible for my own and others' work performance. I want to be successful in my role. I realize that all of the important work of this enterprise is done by and through people. I can't succeed unless my teammates—above me, below me, and beside me—also are successful.*

*I appreciate that I do not have other people's answers. They will become more effective if they are permitted to discover them for themselves. However, I have experience, wisdom, insights, and good ideas to pass along.*

*I may be able to help others achieve their goals even more effectively if I share what I know and what I see. I can use coaching as the process of empowering and inspiring others to higher levels of performance.*

*Therefore, I choose to be a Transformational Coach.*

*If you think you can,
you can; if you think
you can't, you're right.*
**Mary Kay Ash**

This leads us to a Transformational Coach's credo, which includes the following beliefs:

- People are inherently good and they want to contribute

- People are doing the best they can with what they know and are aware of at any given moment

- People make mistakes, but most do not set out to make mistakes on purpose

- Mistakes can be framed positively as learning opportunities for everybody on the team
- Most people's limiting beliefs about their capacities and capabilities keep them from accomplishing more than they do
- Because most work is done by, through, and with the cooperation of people, transforming their individual effectiveness will transform the performance of the team
- People support the changes and commitments that they create, not the ones forced on them
- Unnecessary control is resented; people prefer to be "led" rather than "managed"
- Outside input from anybody is most helpful when it is really desired
- Coaches can build strong trusting relationships by being open and honest in owning and disclosing their thoughts and feelings
- People's feelings must not be ignored; a holistic view of people allows one to see the whole person
- People appreciate clear, honest feedback delivered in a straightforward manner
- People really do want to improve

All these beliefs can be summed up in a Transformational Coach's version of the "golden rule": a coach has *positive regard* for others. This is the attitude that typifies Transformational Coaching.

The challenge is to suspend our beliefs that block us from becoming coaches. When we consciously explore and replace our limiting belief systems, our energy, tone, and intention shift. It is a journey and it is well worth the effort.

❧

*You've got to keep talking to your people. You've got to keep
believing in them. You must be a confidence builder.*

*I try to refrain from using the words
"can't, won't, I don't know, maybe."*

*I want my men to say "I can, I will, I must, I shall, I know."*

*You have to always try to do everything you can to help them maintain
their confidence level. Put positive pictures in the minds of your staff.
Your attitude is critical.*

**Tommy Lasorda**

*Communicate unto the other person that which you would want him to communicate unto you if your positions were reversed.*

**AARON GOLDMAN**

# Communication Filters

## Distortion, Ego, and All That Stuff

*I know that you think you understand what you heard me say,*
*but I'm not sure you realize that what I said was not what I meant.*

**Unknown**

Maybe you have been in a relationship or worked in an organization in which communication was simple, clear, direct, and spotless. I never have. Communicating in all areas of our lives, personal and professional, is always a challenge. Because communication forms the basis for the Transformational Coaching process, it is important to understand it.

Human beings need to connect with one another intellectually, emotionally, spiritually, and physically. Communication is the word we use to describe the process of making and keeping this connection. If it is such a powerful and basic need, why is it so complicated?

# How Filters Distort Communication

According to research, only 7 percent of the objective message communicated is composed of spoken words. The remaining 93 percent is made up of "style," or meta-communication: tone of voice (38 percent) and body language (55 percent). Ideally, what one attempts to communicate, both verbally and nonverbally, is transmitted unimpeded and uncorrupted to the receiver or "hearer."

*Total Communication:*
*7% spoken words*
*38% tone of voice*
*55% body language*

Unfortunately it hardly ever happens that way.

Each individual has created (with the assistance of an ego) a reality—a way of looking at and interpreting life and the world—that is separate and distinct from all others. This reality consists of the total of all the experiences and conditioning each person absorbed from his or her socialization, the development of the genetic heritage he or she carries from birth, and the choices he or she made along the way. These separate realities act as "communication filters."

Communication filters distort the clarity of a message the way a prism or a camera filter bends or distorts light. They operate at both the transmission and reception points—that is, they affect how you say what you say *and* how I hear it.

The following shows how communications are distorted between people. As the group becomes larger, the potential for confusion and chaos rises exponentially as each person's filters distort group communications in unpredictable ways.

*Filters Block Effective Communication*

As we have seen, the key to Transformational Coaching is to create a shared understanding. Your personal effectiveness as a coach—and your ability to communicate clearly—will be dramatically affected by your ability to understand and appreciate your own filters and the filters of others. You need to know how they operate and you need to master the skills to compensate for their distorting effects.

## The Primary Communication Filters

There are three primary groupings of communication filters: mental state, emotional state, and the current state of the relationship.

### Mental State

Mental state refers to our frame of mind during the communication experience—for example, our relative feeling of optimism or pessimism. Mental-state filters mostly affect our internal processing of information.

Your state of mind also includes your current focus or awareness. When your mental state is clear—or at least relatively uncluttered—you can focus in spite of distractions and remain alert to moment-to-moment experiences. An uncluttered state of mind allows you to sort through and understand communication.

Mental-state filters include assumptions, intentions or hidden agendas, beliefs, and judgments of others and self.

### ASSUMPTIONS

One of the great disappointments in business (and personal) relationships that often leads to their demise is unmet expectations on one or both sides. Expectations are rooted in assumptions, and assumptions are so much a part of the fabric of our roles and responsibilities as to be invisible. They look like facts: "Everybody knows that we only use twenty-pound bond. I was sure you knew that. Anybody who would use fifty-pound bond must be irresponsible, because we all know the consequences."

It takes concentration and constant self-examination to become aware of our own assumptions. If they remain unconscious and unexpressed, people become disappointed and frustrated, and performance suffers.

Assume nothing.

### INTENTION AND HIDDEN AGENDA

We are often unaware of what motivates our behavior—our intention or our personal agenda. If we remain unconscious to our underlying needs and desires, we give our habits and conditioning control over our behaviors. We become more reactive, and less able to respond appropriately or effectively.

Transformational Coaches learn to consciously monitor their intentions. We can accomplish this by asking ourselves, *"In this moment and in this communication, what is my purpose?"* This simple reflection can lead us to discover our true motivations, and to realize we have more choices.

We can choose to disclose our experience that led up to this moment, thus using it as a way to authentically describe our needs, wants, and desires. Or, if we discover our intention/purpose is unhealthy, inappropriate, or dark in nature, we can rethink it and choose a course of action that better suits us and the relationship.

The primary benefit of becoming clear on our intention and personal agenda is that this "mindfulness" provides us with a wider range of possibilities. If we can discover them for ourselves, we can help others do the same. In this way, we use intention and personal agenda to learn about ourselves, others, and how to better forward-the-action together.

## BELIEFS

Beliefs are the conclusions we draw (usually over a lifetime) about our experiences. Our belief systems comprise our personal values as well as the cultural norms and extensive set of rules on which we base value judgments. Our belief systems either limit our thinking and action or empower them.

People seem to operate under one of two major postures in life: to protect or defend themselves against the world or to live, learn, laugh, and love their way through life (the Four L's).

The protector's approach to life is closed, resistant to change, and often overreactive to life situations. People with this life posture are difficult to coach and do not make very good coaches themselves.

People who approach life through the Four L's tend to be more open, resilient, and receptive to the people around them. These people are more likely to be open to change, easy to communicate with, and receptive to coaching. They probably also make the best coaches.

## JUDGMENTS OF SELF AND OTHERS

Humans have a cognitive ability to discern; unfortunately, we frequently apply this talent to making negative judgments about others. We stereotype and categorize people who are different from us, making them or ourselves somehow wrong. In either case, we lose. If we think that other people are better than we are, we feel defective, deficient, or somehow "less than." If we think that we are better than others, we feel arrogant and self-important and often behave in condescending ways.

*Suspicion ain't proof.*
**Charles and
Edith Seashore
What Did You Say?**

The judgments we make reflect our internal communications (self-talk) regarding our self-esteem. For someone with low self-esteem, it may be difficult to accept praise from others for a job well done. Because the mind cannot hold two opposing thoughts simultaneously (a condition called "cognitive dissonance"), a person with low self-esteem resolves the tension by discounting the positive input that does not match the self-perception.

As you can imagine, it is almost impossible for a person in this situation to be very open to the process of being reinforced with appreciative feedback, let alone to be an effective coach for others. (See Chapter 14 for more on healing and self-esteem.)

Projection is a very powerful version of judgment that heavily influences the quality of our relationships. In projection, we assume that what is true for, or of, us is also true for, or of, other people. Although most people engage in projection to some degree, the issue is whether or not we are aware of it and how much we allow it to distort our perceptions of others. Projection may be the basis for empathy. For example, if I judge your action as selfish, I can ask myself how I am also selfish (on occasion) and find compassion for both of us since that is part of the human experience. I do not believe that I can see anything in another that I do not have an experience of in myself.

## Emotional State

Our emotional states are heavily affected by our mental functioning. Research has shown a strong link between the quality of our thinking processes and our resulting emotional states.

Emotional states clearly affect the communication process. Different levels of negative feelings include insecurities, threats, stress, fear, ego needs (the need for approval or connection, the need to be perfect, the need to be right), and unhealed wounds that may reopen during the course of the interaction. On the positive side, joy, delight, hopeful expectations, and laughter change our moods and affect us as well.

*People are disturbed not by events but by their interpretations of these events.*

**Epictetus**

When we are in a good mood and feeling buoyant, we are often more resourceful, easygoing, and open to change. At the other extreme, feeling insecure, threatened, and self-conscious usually makes us difficult to work with; we are more likely to feel threatened by change and may be caught up in protective or defensive behaviors. From a coaching standpoint, it is extremely critical to monitor not only our own emotional states, but those of our coachees.

## The Current State of the Relationship

Relationships with others are unavoidable; none of us works in a vacuum. The quality of relationships within work teams has

a tremendous effect on the effectiveness of individuals, the performance of the teams, and the success of organizations. Relationships are the foundation of all human enterprise.

Negative feelings between the coach and the coachee, unfin-
ished business, emotional residue, unresolved conflicts—all can
poison an interaction.

Transformational Coaches focus their energy on developing
clean, honest, and helpful working relationships within and across
teams and on coaching others to do the same.

## The Antidote: Becoming Centered

"Centered" refers to a self-aware, less reactive state of mind in
which we become really tuned in to our personal filters. Given
that we probably can not get rid of all of our own communication
filters—and we certainly can not rid others of theirs—what does
a coach do about them?

Begin with two steps:

1. Become aware
2. Make it explicit

Effective Transformational Coaches develop an awareness and
an appreciation for their own communication filters and those of
their coachees.

### Becoming Aware

Coaches pay particular attention to:

- Spoken and unspoken role expectations
- Underlying assumptions
- The quality of the relationships between people who need
  to work together
- The degree of openness, trust, and rapport that is main-
  tained in working relationships

As coaches, we can become aware of filters by listening care-
fully and keeping our eyes and hearts open.

Examine your own relationships to see to what extent projection is operating. Someone once said, "If you spot it, you got it." This saying is helpful in developing a modicum of humility. See others as mirrors of yourself; it is healing (and more helpful) to work on *your own* versions of the behaviors that you experience as offensive in others.

With each interaction, be aware of your own agenda and be clear about the goals and outcomes that you are attempting to create.

Make your coaching relationship a safe place in which to discuss beliefs and the implications of those beliefs as they affect the working relationship. This level of dialogue creates an opportunity for people to connect deeply with one another and to develop solid trust.

Manage your mental state. Practice being aware of your mental processes. Unique among the planet's species, humans have the ability to *think about* what they think about. Become aware of what you think about and how you think about it; monitor the effect that these thoughts have on your experience. For example, it is helpful (and maybe amusing) to think of our conditioned, habitual thoughts as uncaged monkeys on a bus. We can get on the bus and try to control the monkeys, but this is futile.

Another choice is to just notice the bus passing by with the monkeys jumping out of control, and remain fascinated about the thought process in a detached way, knowing they are just our thoughts, and refusing to let them rule us. Will Rogers had a saying that ran something like this: "I've had some awful experiences in my life, and most of them didn't happen."

Become aware of the tone you set in your verbal communications—your personal style—and the effect it has on others. Style, when it comes to communications, refers not to *what* we say but *how* we say it. It includes our speaking volume, tone, pitch, and pace.

Become aware of your personal style preferences and those of your coachees. For example, one of the topics for the early coaching meetings ought to be how each person would prefer to be coached—what style works for him or her. Some people want extremely direct communication; some want it fast and to the

point; some prefer their coaching with lots of detail to back it up;
some just want the headlines; some want to share their feelings as
they go along. Effective coaches will honor these requests and see
them as just another way to build rapport.

## Making It Explicit

Explicitly state your intentions and help to bring to the surface
the intentions of others. If you do not state your intentions yourself, you risk people attributing motivations (often negative) to
your actions.

Validate your assumptions. Most of us talk at such a rapid pace
that we skip over the obvious step of clarifying assumptions as we
go.

Ensure a common understanding of the goals and objectives
(what success looks like) and the timetable for completion. Ask
effective questions to align expectations and make sure that a project starts off on the right foot. Listen to the answers. Simple
feedback often gives the coach the clue that he or she and the
coachee are not in agreement or are not making the same assumptions.

Our minds take the current event, pull past experiences from
our memories to create a context, and blend them together to formulate an interpretation of the current event. The mind forms
assumptions, draws conclusions, and creates the basis for our
actions. It happens instantaneously, in about one-tenth of a
nanosecond. To compensate, one of the most effective things a
Transformational Coach can do is to slow down the process of
drawing conclusions and attributing motives. One way is through
effective listening.

Invest time in a listening check. Check out your understanding
by simply asking for validation of what you think you heard. This
simple two-step process will help: First, summarize in your own
words what you heard. "This is what I heard you say…(summarize what you heard)…"; then ask, "Is that what you meant? Do I
have it right? Am I understanding you correctly?"

Make frequent use of specific agreements that articulate mutual
commitments. Coaches can contract to establish the terms of the

coaching relationship and the commitment each will keep in that relationship. Create a joint mission (and goals) with your coachee so that you share a common purpose in working together.

Develop your communication skills. Coach others to develop theirs. Communication skills include clear speaking, effective use of language, reflective listening, and engaging in dialogue. The coach also has a responsibility to provide feedback to people who may need skill development to enhance their effectiveness.

## The Ego vs. The Self

One of the most interesting aspects of the human condition is that we all have egos.[12] Egos allow us to grow into separate, distinct, and independently functioning human beings, each with its own identity. Ego strength is necessary to survive. That's the good news.

The bad news is that the ego's belief in the self as separate, distinct, and independent extracts a price from us. It creates an illusion of separateness that limits our ability to connect with others. Left to its own devices, an ego can begin to rule a self. The self becomes ego-driven.

At its best, being ego-driven means that we make judgments about ourselves compared to others that leave us feeling either better-than or worse-than. In either case, we feel separate and disconnected. At worst, we live in fear of losing control. We work to preserve our self-images, then we react defensively to protect ourselves.

"Centered" can also be described as a state of mind in which one becomes detached from the ego's preoccupation with seeing itself as the center of the universe. The next page lists the differences between these two states of mind.

The two columns could also be labeled Unhealthy and Healthy, Dysfunctional and Functional, Ineffective and Effective. The most helpful place from which effective coaching occurs is from a centered state.

I believe that the term "centered" will be unfamiliar for some readers of this book. But I also believe that everyone has had the

[12] For a wonderful treatment of ego, read *There Is Nothing Wrong With You* by Cheri Huber (Mountain View, CA: Keep It Simple Books, 1993).

*Healing comes only from that which leads the patient beyond himself and beyond his entanglements with ego.*

**Carl Jung**

## Differences Between Ego-Driven and Centered States

| An Ego-Driven State | A Centered State |
| --- | --- |
| Self-Conscious | Self-Aware |
| Separate | Connected |
| Busy mind | Quiet mind |
| Righteous/Always right | Learning/Beginners mind |
| Wanting attention | Paying attention |
| Fixing others | Accepting others |
| Invested in image | Authentic/Real |
| Takes things personally | Detached |
| Resistant | Reflective |
| Denial/Stuck | Accepting/Open to change |
| Driven by fear | Choosing from love |
| Closed | Open |
| Locked into expectations | Open to interpretations |
| Arrogant | Humble |
| Critical/Judgmental | Accepting/Discerning |
| Resentful | Respectful |
| Hurried/No Patience | Patient/No Hurry |
| Talks a lot | Listens a lot |
| Seeks approval | Seeks truth |
| Insecure/Anxious | Secure/Confident |
| Getting (Gives to get) | Giving (Unconditionally serves) |
| Absent-minded | Mindful |
| Protective | Purposeful |
| Controlling | Nurturing |
| Triggered/Angry | Grateful |
| Follows external authority | Follows innate wisdom |
| Analyzing/Comparing | Noticing "what is so" |
| Striving | Graceful |
| Pushing | Allowing |
| Cautious | Creative |
| Being perfect | Being "in process" |
| Not making mistakes | Not telling lies |
| Projecting | Reflecting |

experience of being "centered." For some, it may be in prayer; for others, meditation provides this peaceful, restful state. Others have experienced it walking in nature, or looking at a magnificent sunset or sunrise. It is when you have a felt sense that: *"There is more to life than it appears; Everything is as it should be; I am going to be all right; This discomfort, too, shall pass."* It is different for different people.

What is also common is for this experience of feeling centered to inevitably be disrupted by our ego's conditioned thoughts shouting at us: *"Something is really wrong with me; I am not going to make it; People should act better than they do; They are out to get me; I do not deserve this."*

## Aids To Becoming More Centered

Accepting this concept as helpful and actually moving to it are two different things. The rest of this chapter focuses on this transition.

### The Mood Map

Mental and emotional functioning are closely connected. Our conscious awareness and the quality of our thinking directly influence our emotional and feeling responses. To the extent that we are able to become aware of this relationship and begin to manage the thinking processes for ourselves, we may be able to function at higher levels of emotional health and performance.[13]

The Mood Map, on the next page, can help.

Reading from left to right on the Mood Map, we see the causal connection between our thinking state and our feeling response, which influences our behaviors, which affect our outcomes. In addition, there is a vertical dimension, with upper and lower levels of thinking that manifest unique outcomes.

It is helpful to use the Mood Map in reverse, as a guide to understanding how your thinking impacts your personal effectiveness. Think of a personal or work situation in which you might have strong feelings. Start on the right side of the map by locating the ROI that you are currently experiencing. Next, check to see if the behavioral pattern is similar to what is indicated in the

[13] For more background, read *Sanity, Insanity, and Common Sense,* by Rick Suarez, Roger C. Mills, and Darlene Stewart (New York: Ballantine Books, 1987).

## The Mood Map—from Thoughts to Reality

| | Thinking State (Beliefs and and Attitudes) | Feeling State (Emotional Response) | Behaviors (Actions and Reactions) | ROI (Results, Outcomes, and Impacts) |
|---|---|---|---|---|
| **HIGHER STATES ▲** | **"I'm resourceful"** Up to my life Worthy Enough | Confident Inspired Eager Optimistic | Graceful Creative Purposeful Responsive | Joy Peace Bliss Resiliency |
| | **"I'm grateful"** Appreciative Unique Precious | Generous Empowered Abundant Positive | Contribute Give Support Thanks | Fulfillment Intimacy Safety Partnership |
| | **"I'm curious"** Wonderment Interested Inviting | Open Accepting Fascinated Surprised | Ask questions Attentive listening Disclosing Respectful | Learning Connection Trust Rapport |

**↕ CHOICE ↕**

| | | | | |
|---|---|---|---|---|
| **LOWER STATES ▼** | **"I'm separate"** You vs. Me Judgment Comparing | "Better Than" (Arrogant) "Less Than" (Resentful) | Critical/Discount Judgment/Blame Defend/Protect Stuff | Tension Distance Withdrawal Compliance |
| | **"I am my role"** I am identified Take it personally Win/Lose | Insecure Threatened Suspicious Afraid | Attributions Resistance Attack Sabotage | Conflict Struggle Politics War |
| | **"I'm powerless"** I can't I'm stuck I'm helpless | Depressed Out of control Alone Despair | Frozen Wait/Hope Negative Reactionary | Victim Sinking Others control you Giving Up |

Behavior column. Reading to the left, determine whether the associated Feeling State may underlie those behaviors and the extent to which your Thinking State has brought about the results. If you find connections and determine a causal relationship, work on the left side of the map.

Examine, accept, and consciously change (elevate) the beliefs, thoughts, and attitudes that may be creating the context for your present result. High-performing individuals seem to have high-performance belief systems that they consciously develop, monitor, and feed with helpful and powerful thoughts. This starts with high levels of self-awareness.

Many of my life experiences pretty well match the words on the Mood Map, which are meant to be indicators only. Your personal life experiences may match to a greater or lesser degree. Play with this Mood Map and see what connections you can make as you coach people (and are coached). Keep it light. If it works, use it. You may find that you and others are able to see issues and problems more clearly, and to more quickly discover solutions, when you are experiencing a more elevated, healthier state of mind.

## Your Spiritual Path

Many of the world's spiritual practices lead to a release of the ego's grip on personality and to finding one's "center." Some of the most profound movement I have made on this journey has come from consciously attempting to bring more of my heart into my relationships and coaching practice. As I have worked on my own spiritual growth and emotional healing, it has become clear to me that egocentricity drives the negative aspects of the communication filters. Ego is the "mother of all filters." My ego causes the greatest amount of communication distortion and dysfunction in my personal and professional relationships.

There are many paths to enlightenment, and enlightenment is really what I am talking about. This is important to coaching because the Transformational Coach learns to come from a self-aware (centered) place so that he or she can focus on the other person. As a coach, I can not do that very well if I am preoccupied with my ego needs. To become the powerful and magnificent coach I am capable of becoming, I must learn how to detach, to set my needs aside, and to listen deeply with my heart.

When I am relatively detached from what is going on around me, I do not take things personally and I am better able to give other people the benefit of the doubt. I am more able to assume that people are truly innocent in their motivations. I am less likely to believe that people set out with the intention to make mistakes or to ruin my day. I am more likely to choose to believe that most people are trying to do the best job they know how to do, with what they are aware of at the time.

There are many spiritual paths available to us. We choose the one that most honors our deepest sense of who we are. What has been important for me on my journey has been the connection between being on a spiritual path (that is, having a spiritual context within which to live my life) and coaching. I encourage you to discover the connection that brings you joy in this transformational way of working with people.

*We meet ourselves time
and again in a
thousand disguises
on the path of life.*
**Carl Jung**

*For one human being to love another:
that is perhaps the most difficult of our tasks,
the ultimate test and proof,
the work for which all other work is but preparation.*
**Rainer Maria Rilke**

*Using feminine principles in business is wonderful—leading a company with gut feelings, instinct, intuition, passion. Very strong female ethics revolve around the concept of caring and sharing....*

**ANITA RODDICK**

# Coaching Styles

## *What Works When with Whom*

A discussion of behavioral styles is important and relevant to coaching. The personal behavioral patterns we each develop as we mature represent other filters through which we interact with the world and everyone in it. We all have a unique set of characteristics and attributes that defines our personalities. Since the dawn of time, man has sought to understand and explain these differences among people.

Early astrology taught that the alignment of the heavens created the foundation for human behavior. This system postulated twelve signs in four groups: earth, fire, air, and water. Hippocrates refined the system to four temperaments: choleric, phlegmatic, sanguine, and melancholy.

In 1923, based on scientific-research methods, Carl Jung described these four styles as intuitor, thinker, feeler, and sensor. Since then, numerous brain and behavioral studies have added to our understanding about why people act and interact the way they do.

**Behavioral Styles Down Through the Ages**

| Source | The Four Categories | | | |
|---|---|---|---|---|
| Astrology | Water | Fire | Air | Earth |
| Hippocrates | Melancholy | Sanguine | Phlegmatic | Choleric |
| Jung | Feeler | Intuitor | Thinker | Sensor |
| Merrill/Wilson/Allessandra | Amiable | Expressive | Analytical | Driver |
| Performax | Steadiness | Influence | Compliance | Dominance |
| Cathcart/Allessandra | Relater | Socializer | Thinker | Director |
| Crane Consulting* | Collaborating | Creating | Clarifying | Conducting |

*Note: The "verbal noun" (gerund) form of these words is used to discourage the labeling that occurs with nouns.

## The Four Behavioral Styles

Style can be distinguished on the continua of assertiveness and emotiveness. The the four basic styles shown at right reflect the contributions that individuals bring to a team. I call them Collaborating, Creating, Clarifying, and Conducting and have selected these names to capture the true gift each style contributes.

The quality of rapport and connection the coach and coachee develop in their coaching relationship has a profound impact on the effectiveness of Transformational Coaching. Understanding stylistic differences is a key to creating more rapport. Both the coach and the coachee can learn to use the information from these behavioral styles to their advantage. The operative principle for all is the same: Know your own and your coachee's style and be flexible with your coaching approach so that you can match the coachee's style.

## The Four Behavioral Styles

| | **Collaborating** | | **Creating** | |
|---|---|---|---|---|
| **High** | **STRENGTHS** | **WEAKNESSES** | **STRENGTHS** | **WEAKNESSES** |
| | Team player | Non confrontive | Enthusiastic | Poor follow-through |
| | Sensitive | Overly compliant | Creative | Impulsive |
| | Flexible | Overly emotional | Spontaneous | Misses details |
| | Patient | Can't say no | Dynamic | Poor planner |

| | **Clarifying** | | **Conducting** | |
|---|---|---|---|---|
| | **STRENGTHS** | **WEAKNESSES** | **STRENGTHS** | **WEAKNESSES** |
| | Systematic | Data bound | Independent | Autocratic |
| | Objective | Risk averse | Initiator | Insensitive |
| | Thorough | Tedious | Disciplined | Impatient |
| | Accurate | Perfectionist | Organized | Poor listener |

EMOTIVENESS ▲

Low

Low      **ASSERTIVENESS ▶**      High

## The Collaborating Style:
### Low Assertiveness, High Emotiveness

**KEY STRENGTHS**

People who have this style are sensitive to and aware of people's feelings, flexible in finding win/win solutions to problems, good team members, and patient in working with people.

**KEY WEAKNESSES—POTENTIAL AREAS FOR COACHING**

Collaborators may find it difficult to confront others, they tend to be overly compliant and can be overly emotional, and they find it difficult to say "no" to people.

### THE COLLABORATING STYLE AS COACH

The collaborating coach is usually very trustworthy and in touch with the coachee's feelings and needs, but may have a difficult time confronting tough issues in performance or the relationship. Collaborating coaches may, therefore, be too patient with their coachees. They may use indefinite words in dialogue with them, creating confusion and lack of a sense of urgency for the coachee. They may never proceed to Forwarding the Action.

Collaborating coaches can learn from conducting coaches (the style diagonally across the matrix) about being assertive enough to name the issues. They need to learn that it is possible to be supportive while simultaneously challenging coachees to be accountable for results. Using documented performance-improvement plans helps coaches with this style to identify and address the issues.

### TIPS FOR COACHING THE COLLABORATING COACHEE

To coach a collaborating person, be *people-focused*: warm, relaxed, involving, caring, inviting, and concerned. Create rapport with a collaborating person by saying something like this:

*"Sally, I have some strong feelings about something that might be negatively affecting the team's ability to work well and I wondered if you would be open to hearing my thoughts on what might help everybody."*

## The Creating Style:
### *High Assertiveness, High Emotiveness*

### KEY STRENGTHS

People who display the creating style tend to be highly energetic and enthusiastic about work, able to generate lots of ideas and options, and highly spontaneous. They use intuitive powers well, are dynamic in speech, and have a flair for the dramatic.

**KEY WEAKNESSES—POTENTIAL AREAS FOR COACHING**

Such people tend to be impulsive and overly reactive, tend to neglect details, are relatively unfocused on follow-through, and are not good at planning ahead.

**THE CREATING STYLE AS COACH**

Although good at talking on their feet, creating-style coaches are frequently so spontaneous as to be unprepared; they often do not have the facts the coachee needs. Their extreme optimism may make it difficult for them and their coachees to see the reality of a given coaching situation. As a result, they may fail to focus on real issues and obstacles to progress. Talking in "rough draft" is a characteristic of this style, a trait that others may perceive as wishy-washy and confusing. Follow-through may also be a challenge, as the creating person is quickly ready to move on to new things.

A coach who has the creating style can learn from the (diagonal) clarifying style. Creating-style coaches need to learn to be more thorough in their coaching and to make sure that they are adequately prepared for the coachee's need for specifics. They should concentrate on slowing down and reflectively listening through the feedback loop to make sure that they connect with the coachee and his or her point of view before offering ideas. Creating-style coaches need to remember to keep their agreements to meet and follow up with their coachees.

**TIPS FOR COACHING THE CREATING STYLE COACHEE**

To coach a person who displays the creating style, be *idea-focused*: enthusiastic, expressive, friendly, flexible, open to possibilities, and a big-picture thinker. Try saying something like the following in order to build rapport:

> *"Fred, I've got a fantastic idea about how you might blow this year's goals out of the water! Have you got a minute to see how this might fit into your business plan?"*

## The Conducting Style:
### High Assertiveness, Low Emotiveness

**KEY STRENGTHS**

Conductors are able to take charge and initiate projects, think independently, are highly disciplined, focused on results, and good at organizing people and tasks.

**KEY WEAKNESSES—POTENTIAL AREAS FOR COACHING**

Conductors may be insensitive to other people's feelings and needs, they tend toward autocratic decision making, may be impatient, and tend not to listen well.

**THE CONDUCTING STYLE AS COACH**

The conducting-style coach is really good at organizing things but is often insensitive to the fact that people desire leadership, not moment-to-moment management. Autopilot for the conducting approach is command and control and micro-management. Conductors tend to coach only in the measurable-results arena and leave out the relationship realm. Telling is comfortable for the conducting coach; asking effective questions and listening for the responses is really challenging work.

Lessons for conductors come from the style most unlike them: the collaborative coach. Conductor coaches need to balance coaching on the objective, results side of the ledger with proper attention to the people side. They need to learn to listen with their hearts to what their coachees are saying, not just to focus on the numbers.

**TIPS FOR COACHING THE CONDUCTING COACHEE**

To coach a conducting personality, be *results-focused:* clear, concise, focused, relevant, decisive, and efficient. Enhance rapport with a conducting personality by saying something such as:

> *"Doris, I know you are pushing really hard to get this operations project off the ground, with stellar results. I think I see something that might be in your way. Would you want to discuss it?"*

## The Clarifying Style:
### Low Assertiveness, Low Emotiveness

#### KEY STRENGTHS

Clarifiers are very systematic and deliberate in their thinking and planning, they are able to maintain an objective perspective based on facts, and they are very thorough, complete, and accurate in their work.

#### KEY WEAKNESSES—POSSIBLE AREAS FOR COACHING

Clarifiers can be tedious and boring in their interactions with others; perfectionism tends to create analytical paralysis. This type of person tends to be too conservative and risk-averse in decision making and execution, and gets too caught up in the numbers of life and work.

#### THE CLARIFYING STYLE AS COACH

In striving to understand thoroughly, clarifying coaches tend to go so slowly that some coachees run out of patience. If the audience is lost, the message is lost. In addition, clarifying coaches need to make it okay for people to make mistakes (provided that they learn and share their learning with others). Thoroughness can come off as nit-picky, so coaches with this style should remember to lighten up a little.

The clarifying coach's opportunities to become more effective come from the strengths of the (diagonally situated on the matrix) creative style. Clarifying coaches should move along at a fast enough tempo to keep their coachees' interest. These coaches should remember to keep coaching focused on the coachees' goals, rather than on their own interests. Clarifying coaches must strive for balance between the details and the big picture, without losing sight of the purpose. They need to watch their tendency to become preachy (teachers of lessons) when dealing with adults.

#### TIPS FOR COACHING THE CLARIFYING COACHEE

When coaching a clarifying person, be *data-focused*: specific, thorough, prepared, accurate, rational, and orderly. Build rapport with communications such as:

*"Paul, these data seem inconsistent with what I thought you were look-
ing for. I have two ideas that would improve the quality and timeliness of
the team's efforts. I need fifteen minutes to discuss this with you. Can we
meet at four-thirty today?"*

## What To Remember About Behavioral Styles

It is easy to misuse any tool. Most people resent being labeled or
placed in a box. When I cover this material on behavioral styles
in workshops, I ask people to remember the following points:

- Style is a preference and a choice. It is not what people are.
  Each of us have some of the skills and abilities from all four
  styles.

- No one style is better. Any style can be effective in almost
  any situation. It is the situation and the person with whom
  you are interacting that determines the approach that may
  work best. Flexibility is the key.

- Weaknesses are merely overdeveloped strengths. As you
  become aware of your preferences, try seeing your
  strengths as blind spots that filter out other possibilities.
  Continually expand the range and the flexibility of your
  style.

- Each style has its own language, beliefs, and skills. Each
  style is effective. Each style has a place on the team. High-
  performance teams value and blend all the styles.

- Do not take this structured framework too seriously. Do
  not use it to evaluate and separate people into categories.
  Use it to connect with and value them.

## Coaching and Generational Differences

There are three distinct generations working side by side in most
organizations. This has been true for decades, but it is especially
significant now.

## Contrasting the Generations—Three Generations in U.S. Society Today

|  | Traditionalists<br>"The Silent Generation" | Boomers<br>"Yuppies" | X'ers<br>"Yiffies" |
|---|---|---|---|
| Birth Years | 1925-1945 | 1946-1964 | 1965-1980 |
| Conditioning Years | 30's-40's | 50's-60's | 70's-80's |
| World Frame | Depression, WWII<br>Struggle and sacrifice<br>Delayed gratification | Sexual revolution<br>Economic expansion<br>Abundance, Spending | MTV, AIDS epidemic<br>Cynical<br>Grim economic reality |
| Family Structure | Nuclear | Divorced | Latch key kids |
| Who, What Is Trusted | Doctors | Feelings | Technology |
| Music Favored | Swing<br>Old standards<br>Elevator music | Rock & roll<br>Jazz<br>New age | Rap, Punk<br>Heavy metal<br>Alternative |
| Work Ethic | Work hard<br>Pay dues<br>Keep head down<br>"I am my job" | Climb the ladder<br>Build career<br>Workaholics<br>"Work is my life" | Distrust big business<br>Nine to five<br>Independence<br>"Work gives me a life" |
| Attitude Toward Authority | Respect it | Question it | Challenge it |
| Management Style Favored | Command and control | Collaborative | Entrepreneurial |
| Loyalty To | My company | My profession | My family |
| Organizational Structure Favored | Formal<br>Hierarchical | Informal<br>Accessible | Unconventional<br>Connected network |
| How Job Is Valued | Stability, Security | Career growth | Stepping stone |
| How Communication Is Perceived | No news is good news | Any news is good news | Need news, straight talk, and feedback |
| How Organizational Life Is Dealt with | Dedicated<br>Committed<br>Social contract | Disillusioned<br>Downsized<br>Broken agreement | Realistic<br>Risk takers<br>No agreement |
| What Is Resented | Change<br>Lack of respect | Control<br>Slackers | Corporate politics<br>Boomers clogging the system |
| What Is Valued | Stability<br>Respect<br>Trust<br>Hard work<br>Loyalty | Variety<br>Achievement<br>Actualization<br>Career<br>Flexibility | Learning<br>Quality of life<br>Involvement<br>Stimulation<br>Fun |

Sources are cited in Appendix Two (page 219)

The three generations are the Traditionalists, the Baby Boomers, and Generation X. Each grew up and was inculturated at a different time in this country's history, over a span of sixty years that has included huge social, economic, and political shifts in the United States and the world. As a result, each generation has embraced different values, beliefs, and paradigms.

The differences have implications for coaches. Coaching people from these three generations creates unique challenges in establishing and maintaining rapport and connection and accomplishing the important work of the company. It is easy to stereotype others because of their age, gender, race, style, and perceived values. Our perceptions of generational differences are manifestations of the "judgments" filter. Coaches must become aware of this potentially unhelpful aspect of human nature and consciously choose to value differences, especially those based on the richness of diversity available to us today. In high-performing environments, team members consciously embrace and cultivate the diversity of the team's members and view their differences as strengths. See "Contrasts in the Generations," on the previous page, for an outline of the differences among generations.

## Coaching the Traditionalist

People from the Traditionalist generation have been required to deal with more changes than any other generation. The world they grew up in was very different than that of the Boomers or the X'ers. That fact alone is cause for compassion and understanding. Connecting with them is easier when one is:

- Respectful of their experience and values the perspective they bring to the organization
- Patient with and understanding of their resistance to quick changes
- Respectful of their need for orderliness and a clear sense of direction
- Empathic about the emotional effect on them of the changed social contract

- Willing to find ways to enroll them as wise coaches and mentors for the organization.

## Coaching the Boomer

Baby boomers were conditioned in an age of unparalleled economic prosperity. They believe that anything is possible if they throw enough money at it. In an economic age that has richly rewarded individual achievement, Boomers have become caught up in the materialistic pursuit of toys, and many have lost a sense of balance in the process. Approach them with:

- Respect for their achievements and the range of choices they may have become used to exercising

- Appreciation for their energy and commitment to working hard for their results

- The willingness to help them create more balance in their lives

- A challenge to collaborate with and involve those around them in solving the problems of today's organizations

- An intent to involve them in articulating the direction of the organization, especially the implementation of change initiatives

- Offers to enroll them as coaches in the process of change

## Coaching the X'ers

Many people in the younger generation of workers have grown up in broken homes and have learned to be relatively independent about having their needs met. They have developed the ability to discern lies and half-truths quickly. They make up their own minds about things, rejecting many of the beliefs that the Boomers took at face value. In coaching X'ers, one needs to:

- Respect the extraordinary times and life experiences that shaped their thinking and beliefs (AIDS and computers, for example)

- Understand that their relative lack of attachment and excitement about material things may come from having so much

- Tell them the truth, including placing boundaries around what cannot be talked about

- Provide career-enriching opportunities to satisfy their passion for learning

- Honor the sense of balance and respect for family that they bring to work

- Spend as much time as necessary orienting them to the organization's culture and be clear about your expectations

## Using the Knowledge

Some of the tips in this chapter may assist you in connecting with potential coachees. But remember, not everybody fits a mold. I am the father of Generation-X kids and I have had some struggles in understanding and staying connected with them. The information in the table "Contrasting the Generations" has helped me to better appreciate the world in which my children grew up. It has given me more to talk about and share with them. I hope it has the same effect for you with people at home or at work.

We always need to find ways to connect and collaborate with people to achieve the goals of the organization. It is a strategic error to maintain emotional distance from people just because they are different, because they do not look like us, like different music, or are "bugged" or excited by different things. If they work for our company, they are on our team. *They* are not the enemy; the competition is. A Transformational Coach knows this and facilitates connection at every opportunity.

❧

*To be surprised, to wonder, is to begin to understand.*
**Jose Ortega Y Gasset**

*The best and most beautiful things in the world cannot be seen or even touched. They must be felt with the heart.*

HELEN KELLER

# Miscellaneous Coaching Tips

## A Collection of Ideas and Hints

Although coaching is more than a technique, there are some specifics to keep in mind to keep the process on track. This chapter provides a number of helpful tips for both giving and receiving coaching that will make the process easier and more successful.

## Giving Coaching

If your coaching comes from the heart, the chances are that it will be transformational for you and for your coachee. Check this list of tips from time to time just to make sure that you are on the right track.

### Remember Your "ABCs"

ABC stands for "**A**sk **B**efore **C**oaching"—an easy way to remember that requesting and receiving permission is critical to the Transformational Coaching process. The danger of "dumping" feedback on people when it is convenient for you is that it may not be convenient or the right time or place for them. Asking first is a clear sign of respect for the coachee and will always serve you well in building and maintaining trust in the relationship.

### Make It Mutual

For the coaching process to achieve its full potential to connect people in an environment of trust, respect, and rapport, the coach must frequently ask for coaching from the coachee. This demonstrates the coach's intention to learn and grow as a teammate by creating the sense of a level playing field. It must become normal for a coachee—often a subordinate in the organization—to offer coaching to the coach.

One of the things that the coach can ask for feedback on is the work relationship with the coachee. Work performance is another area of inquiry. The coaching process itself is another topic for feedback. Ask questions such as:

- "What's working?"
- "What's not working?"
- "What should I do more of?" "Less of?"
- "What should I stop doing?" "Start doing?"

This gives the coachee an opportunity to share his or her thoughts and feelings and contribute to improving the process. Just as important, it identifies anything that may be keeping your coaching from being its best.

### Be Conversational in Tone

*The primary medium for all coaching interventions is conversation.*

**Robert Hargrove**

A conversational tone is informal, relaxed, good-hearted, easy to listen to, and full of humor. Most people would rather be conversed with than talked at. Many coaches fall into the trap of using a "telling" style of speech. This directive approach should be saved for situations for which it is truly appropriate. Otherwise, you risk coming across as condescending or parental, which interferes with the coaching process.

### Check for Understanding

For any conversation to have the feel of mutual dialogue, both parties should use questions to clarify their understanding throughout the conversation. The coach should take the lead in clarifying not only what has just been said but also what has been heard. The interpretation is critical to creating a shared understanding. Simply saying, "This is what I heard you say. Is that what you meant?" is an easy and effective way to check for understanding.

### Support *Their* Goals

Support the goals of your coachees. U.S. business people are results-focused and bottom-line driven. Most bosses have clear agendas and strong ideas about what must be accomplished and how it should be done that interfere with their ability to listen to people and understand what *their* problems and issues are in achieving the results for which they are accountable. Learn to ask questions and listen deeply to the responses. In this way, you can become more focused on helping people to remove barriers that stand in their way. If a coachee's goals appear to be out of alignment with yours, and that is not appropriate for your work situation, then that requires a different conversation. By all means, hold it soon!

*To love what you do and
feel that it matters—
how could anything
be more fun?*

**Katherine Graham**

### Pay Attention to How It Lands

As you deliver feedback, pay close attention to the coachee's response. Focus on his or her body language, facial expression, and tone of voice. Certain clues tell you how he or she is hearing what you have shared. When you perceive that the person is becoming upset or taking it poorly (usually personally), check to see if he or she is okay and then decide whether to continue or not. Placing yourself in your coachee's shoes and summoning empathy will pay great dividends in the relationship. It is possible to say almost anything to almost anybody if you speak from your heart.

### Share Accountability for Success and Failure

In many corporate cultures, people invest considerable time in placing blame, ducking responsibility, and punishing the guilty. Coaches can change this practice for the entire culture by holding themselves fully accountable for the success of their coachees. Accountability is the empowering attitude through which both people in the relationship accept 100 percent of the responsibility for the success of that relationship and the results that they *jointly* produce. Accountable coaches always seek to understand their effect—positive and negative—on performance and on the working relationship, and then act on the behaviors that are within their control.

### Progress, Not Perfection

Our society values perfection in all things—in faces, bodies, control, parenting, and so on. This is dysfunctional thinking at worst, and it is easy to get caught up in it. *Nobody* is perfect, and no one ever will be. Waiting for a person to perform a task or accomplish a goal without making a single mistake is an unrealistic and unhealthy expectation.

Your job is to encourage and support people in moving in a positive direction. Effective coaches are continually alert to incremental improvements in attitude, behavior, or work processes; they provide recognition to people when they have achieved progress. Stay focused on reinforcing positive progress toward meaningful goals.

### Talk About What Needs To Be

Things will come to your mind from time to time that may seem inappropriate as topics for coaching or personal feedback, for example, bad breath, dandruff, a nervous tick or mannerism, bad table manners, or alcohol abuse. There is almost no topic that cannot be broached under the right conditions, with the right intentions, with the right trusting relationship. This is especially true if you sincerely believe that the information may be relevant, important, or helpful to your coachee. If you believe the behavior in question is adversely affecting or limiting otherwise good performance, find a way to talk about it from your heart.

## Make It "Face Time"

In light of the huge growth in popularity of electronic communications, do not forget the power of face-to-face meetings.
Writing a memo or sending an e-mail message is a distant and
poor substitute for personal communication. Nothing is as powerful as looking another human being in the eyes and having a real
dialogue. That is where the connection happens. If you feel that
you may be starting to lose touch with someone (or you receive
feedback that you are losing touch), pay attention to the processes you are using to maintain your communications.

## Carpé Momento (Seize the Moment)!

Robin Williams' character in *The Dead Poets Society* reminded us
of the importance of *seizing the day* (*carpé diem*). For coaches, the
motto is *carpé momento*—seize the moment. Within the context of
a safe, established coaching relationship, do not be afraid to offer
coaching "in the moment." People who are open to hearing feedback in the heat of the action have an opportunity to respond
instantaneously and change their course of action. This is only
possible, of course, when the coach and the coachee have developed a high level of rapport and can openly and skillfully incorporate feedback received from moment to moment.

## Be Prepared

Being prepared is important in anything you do; it is especially
important to the coaching process. Be very clear about how you
plan to describe, in objective terms, the behavior that you have
observed. Take a few moments before a coaching session to gather your thoughts on suggestions that you want to offer and to
refresh your memory of your personal experiences related to the
current situation.

## Balance Your Feedback

We are psychologically wired to want and need reinforcing
feedback far more than we are able to admit (or get it). No one
receives too much. We especially need lots of support and

encouragement when we try new things in today's changing workplaces.

Make sure that your feedback is lopsided in favor of giving too much appreciative feedback, at least compared to what you have been giving. Provide significantly more supportive and appreciative feedback than you do suggestions for change. Deliver feedback in the following ratio: 80 percent positive and reinforcing—20 percent constructive ideas for change. Transformational Coaching requires a new mindset. Do not focus on errors; focus on progress and on what is going right.

### Be Clear

Many people are pretty good at innuendo, speaking around issues, and speaking in general terms. It is far more helpful to speak clearly and directly in your coaching conversations. Always be clear about your intention and the purpose for the session, and be very specific in the information and ideas you share and direct in the delivery of the message.

### Keep Your Commitments

Do not let other business supersede a commitment for a coaching session unless you first renegotiate the time of the session. Priorities are always changing; that is not the issue. Less experienced coaches sometimes make the mistake of delaying a coaching meeting without explicit communication. First, agree to reschedule the session. Do not assume that you don't have to talk about it. You do, if you are to preserve the trust and respect that you have worked so hard to build. (Here is a Transformational idea: consider sending the signal to the organization that a coaching session *cannot* be changed because it is so important.)

### Transformational Coaching Is a Process

The difference between an event and a process is that events end and processes cycle without end. Transformational Coaching is a process. Many managers make the mistake of saving their coaching for the annual performance evaluation. They operate under the mistaken belief that this is effective and helpful. It is too little, too late.

Progressive organizations and leaders are finding that coaching is a powerful way of staying in continual dialogue about performance-improvement issues throughout the year, quarter, month, and day. People simply need more feedback and ongoing coaching to leverage their performance.

## Transformational Coaching Is Not a Performance Review

Although the process is not a performance review, it supports such processes. If Transformational Coaching is working well in your organization, the coachee will, theoretically, learn nothing new during the actual review. Everything already will have been discussed, so there will be no surprises, just a confirmation of the content of the many dialogues held throughout the performance period.

## See Coaching As Learning

If you are going to be an effective coach, you must do whatever is humanly possible to remove your ego-based filters and protective routines and replace them with an open, learning stance toward life. If you can focus on *learning* about people, processes, or principles every time you coach, you will create more results in the long run. Someone once invited me to exchange my *rightness* for curiosity. It helped. I now invite you to do the same as a way to hold yourself open for learning.

## See Coaching As a Gift

In many cultures, people share gifts when they want to acknowledge one another because they care about one another and wish to demonstrate their caring. The gift is usually a token that will be appreciated by, or is helpful to, the recipient. The feedback in the Transformational Coaching process also can be viewed as a gift. Seen that way, you may be able to hold it more lightly and deliver it with more care.

Consider how you might feel if someone in your organization had feedback for you that might help your performance or working relationships, but he or she withheld it. If you found out, you might feel angry or be disappointed. You might even feel cheated. One good strategy to keep that from happening in your organization is to do your part and offer all the feedback that you have to give. Give it away because you care about the recipient.

## Receiving Coaching

The following story is a powerful example of what can happen when you do not accept feedback.

*A ship was sailing through a heavy fog when its crew sighted a faint light through the mist. The radioman signaled:*

> "Please divert your course 15° to the north to avoid a collision."

*The reply came:*

> "Impossible. Recommend you divert your course 15° to south to avoid a collision."

*The radioman signaled again:*

> "This is a U.S. Navy ship. I say again, divert your course."

*The radioman was surprised to get the response:*

> "No can do. I say again, you divert your course."

*The radioman consulted with the ship's captain. The captain got on the radio and said:*

> **"This is the Captain of a U.S. Navy aircraft carrier. Divert your course now!"**

*The response came:*

> "This is a lighthouse. Your call."

This story can offer some lessons to us as coaches.

- If you can imagine the captain's tone of voice, what message do you think accompanied his or her words?
- What would you project as the emotional state of the captain?
- Have you ever caught yourself acting like the captain?
- What happened the last time you were absolutely certain that you had all the facts you needed to proceed?
- How do you tend to react to those who use a "telling" style?

"Crashing into the lighthouse" is a great metaphor for how we sometimes treat feedback (and the people who bring it).

Receiving feedback is important to Transformational Coaching because of the mutual nature of the coaching relationship. You cannot be an effective coach if you learn how to give feedback but never learn how to graciously accept and respond to it. You are not going to encourage your direct reports to provide feedback if you react badly to it. Don't shoot the messenger.

The following are some tips to remember:

### Be Honest in Giving Permission

In corporations in which hierarchy still prevails, it is standard protocol to defer to your boss. This behavior demonstrates respect for positions above and protects you from the consequences of making waves, stirring the pot, or offending those for whom you work. If your coach (whatever his or her position in the organization) approaches you and asks permission to deliver feedback, it is really more helpful, and more in your own best interest, to give an authentic and sincere response. There will be many times in which you will have a difficult time being receptive to for feedback. If you cannot be emotionally available and present in that moment, thank your coach for the opportunity and defer the conversation to a time that will work better for you. This requires courage but demonstrates the utmost respect for the process. It has to be okay to say no from time to time.

### Receive Feedback As a Gift

This is the flip side of *offering* feedback as a gift. Hold yourself open for the learning opportunities provided by feedback. It is easier to listen to feedback if you visualize an open space in your heart for the information and if you see it as a way to learn about yourself and how you affect others. Regard all input as potentially valuable.

### Do Not Take It Personally

*Remember, no one can make you feel inferior without your consent.*

**Eleanor Roosevelt**

For those of us who have vulnerabilities, unhealed wounds, and emotional sensitivities (in other words, all of us), it is common to feel hurt by even well-intended feedback. Sometimes, we can be emotionally triggered by feedback. When this happens, our egos filter the feedback through our inner critics, who convince us that the feedback is about lack of worth. Many of us come from families—or have worked in environments—in which criticism is an everyday occurrence. There always will be people who have a difficult time changing criticism into feedback, but that is not the issue. The issue is how we interpret and respond to the feedback.

Learn to remind yourself that the feedback may or may not be about you. Your coach, if unaware, unwittingly may be projecting something onto you. Understand that feedback often is more about the person who is delivering it—his or her beliefs, values, assumptions, expectations, and current filters—than it is about your own performance or worth. Cultivating this awareness may allow you to remain detached yet curious about what the feedback tells you about the giver.

### Monitor Your Emotional Reactions

It is your job to pay attention to your own thinking and feeling states at the time that you receive feedback. If you are a normal human being, you may find some feedback to be upsetting and personally offensive. If you find that you are emotionally triggered and beginning to react defensively, or tempted to respond by returning what you perceive to be an attack, just stop. Take a deep breath, remind yourself that receiving feedback is *always* a learning situation (often about the feedback giver), and listen. If you indulge in a negative emotional reaction, you lose your ability to *hear* the feedback. Consider calling a time out and getting back together when you can really listen.

## Focus Your Coach on Your Goals

People tend to deliver feedback on things that are important to them. I am sure that you know people who project their beliefs and judgments about how things ought to be. Frequently, people who have strong agendas do not take the time to find out what is important to you. So it may increase the value of the feedback if, early in the conversation (or the relationship), you let your coach know your goals, objectives, and challenges. This provides an appropriate and clear focus for *most* of the feedback that may follow.

## Clarify Your Feedback

Make sure that you truly understand your coach's meaning. Ask for specific, clear examples to help you to understand the ROI of your actions. An unexpected benefit is that you may develop a deep appreciation for your coach's perspective. Try to stay engaged in dialogue until you can come to appreciate and value the message.

## Take Time To Reflect and Respond (Instead of Reacting)

It is important to not overreact to feedback, regardless of its source. People often have a tendency (especially when feedback comes from a supervisor) to react immediately by promising to change their actions. Be responsive, but be aware that a quick, knee-jerk reaction may not be the best choice.

Remember, you are the one who decides what to do with the feedback and suggestions you receive. Receive the feedback, acknowledge the person giving it, then take time to reflect on the meaning and gradually integrate personal changes that you believe are appropriate, sustainable, and authentic—for you. (You may sometimes choose to change immediately, but it is always your choice.)

On the flip side, you may find yourself reacting to feedback by defending yourself or arguing. This is a wonderful opportunity to breathe deeply and focus on taking in the information. Your objective is to understand the feedback and to consciously choose an appropriate response to it. In the moment of receiving feedback, you need to do nothing but listen calmly. Focus on understanding as much of it as possible and asking any clarifying questions that occur to you.

### Perception Is Reality

The feedback you receive is the subjective reality of another person. It is important to understand and appreciate it in those terms. Whether you *intended* to create the effect or outcome that is being described to you is irrelevant. What is important is to listen and to learn from this person's perception and experience. You need others to share with you what their experience is, good or bad, so that you have the option of considering making a personal change.

### Look for the Kernel

We live in a world that bombards us with enough information to overwhelm most sane people. The burden is on us to figure out what to do with it all. If we are diligent in the that way we handle this information, we can find what is true for us. It takes work to discover the themes in our feedback that relate to our lifelong issues of personal growth and development—the kernel of truth. That is where to focus.

### Let an Acknowledgment "Sink In"

For some strange reason, most of us are pretty good at deflecting acknowledgment, affirmation, and accolades. Somewhere in our Western culture, there is a belief that it is not okay to brag or boast about ourselves and our accomplishments. Research in the last decade regarding development of healthy self-esteem and a strong self-image suggests that it is important for people to learn to accept positive feedback and use it to develop self-esteem. This takes practice. (A deeper discussion of this follows in

Chapter 14.) Try this simple technique. The next time someone offers you positive feedback or a compliment, just say, "Thank you," and smile.

## Always Thank Your Coach

Always demonstrate openness and gratitude for the feedback you have just received, whether it was positive or negative. It does not matter if you agree with it. As a matter of fact, at the time you hear it, you may believe that the feedback is wrong, off base, judgmental, or a result of the coach's projection. Often your coach took a risk to deliver the feedback; acknowledging his or her courage is your way of supporting your coach and developing trust in the relationship.

*Outstanding leaders go out of their way to boost self-esteem of their personnel. If people believe in themselves, it's amazing what they can accomplish.*

**SAM WALTON**

# Self-Esteem and Healing

*You Can't Lead Where You Haven't Traveled*

The challenges that we coaches face at work require us to bring out the best in people and in ourselves. It is impossible to consider being a coach without addressing the subject of self-esteem and emotional healing.

Few judgments we make in life are as important as the ones we make about ourselves. The state of our self-esteem colors all our life experiences. It has a profound effect on our performance at work. It affects how we deal with people, how we operate within our social constructs and work environments and how much we achieve.[14]

Self-esteem includes our internal image of *self-efficacy*—our confidence in our ability to think, act, cope, and face challenges in our lives. Self-esteem also includes *self-respect*, which is our sense of worthiness, importance, and entitlement to assert our needs with others. It sets the context for our life choices.

[14]For more information about self-esteem, read *The Six Pillars of Self-Esteem* by Nathaniel Branden (New York: Bantam Books, 1994).

# Implications for Coaching

*The curious paradox
is that when I accept
myself just as I am,
then I can change.*

**Carl Rogers**

As I have said earlier, the effectiveness of the coaching relationship is based on developing and maintaining the highest levels of trust, honesty, intimacy, and mutual respect with coachees. With regard to self-esteem, a coach's objective is to support and nurture the development of self-esteem and positive self-regard in all aspects of the coaching relationship.

The following attitudes and behaviors will help build your awareness and facilitate the development of healthy self-esteem for both you and your coachees.

### See Others As Unique

There never have been two individuals on the face of the planet, living or dead, who were identical. The fact that we are all unique can form a basis for appreciation and respect for one another. A good coach learns to experience, honor, and celebrate people's uniqueness.

### Invest Time to Appreciate

There is probably a direct relationship between the quality of the coaching relationship and the time invested in the coaching process. Truthful and caring dialogue produces a natural discovery: we learn more about the people with whom we work and therefore have more to appreciate and support in them as human beings and as members of the team.

### Support Others' Life Values and Purposes

A coach can contribute to the discovery and development of another person's life purpose, mission, and values. With high levels of trust, rapport, and permission, a coach can learn about these aspects of the coachee's life. Conversations of this kind may extend into the mentoring arena, and that's okay. It is natural for the coach to want to honor these personal aspects of people when he or she becomes aware of them. These types of conversations flow easily, given the heartfelt connection that develops between the coach and coachee.

## Connect Role and Contribution to Life Purpose

Life purpose can provide the context in which we choose our life's work. A coach who has done this exploratory work in his or her own life will find it easier to help coachees to connect their roles and contributions with their vision of their life purpose. To the extent that people can become clear about the purpose of their lives, the mission they believe they have been placed on this earth to accomplish, and the values they hold close to their hearts, they will have more fulfilling experiences at work, especially if they are able to connect those values and goals to their roles at work. Transformational Coaches are willing to talk about these kinds of things to help people discover such vital connections.

## Stretch and Challenge

Positive self-esteem usually develops in proportion to our accomplishments. Achieving meaningful goals creates a sense of pride and positive image that contributes to our sense of well-being and enhances our ability to perform at higher levels. A good coach will assist the growth and development of a coachee by helping him or her to set goals and objectives that stretch and challenge his or her performance levels. Left to their own devices, people often remain within their personal comfort zones; they may not choose objectives that require their best. An effective coach can help people developmentally by encouraging them to try new things, adopt new roles, and learn new skills.

## Become a Cheerleader

Become a huge fan of other people's work and accomplishments. Reinforce people's achievements in a way that they might not do for themselves. Coaches can develop individual esteem if they seize every opportunity to acknowledge, cheer, and underscore people's successes. In this area, do more, not less.

## Support Learning and the Growth of Self-Esteem

One of the most important questions that a coach can ask is, "What did you learn about yourself?" Keeping the focus on learning helps people to become aware of insights and connections that might otherwise go unnoticed. If, in the course of our over-loaded, stressed-out world of work, we can become conscious of and accept our thoughts, feelings, insights, and attitudes, we become more able to support the growth of positive self-images. Coaches learn to facilitate people's development of new and positive ways of thinking about themselves.

## Team Esteem

Beyond facilitating the development of individual self-esteem, a Transformational Coach plays a major role in contributing to a team's collective self-image—to team esteem. A strong team identity is vital to its ability to perform at high levels. It shows up as team spirit, high camaraderie, mutual support, and lots of good-natured fun. It is an intangible part of the fabric that holds a team together during tough times and it fuels the extraordinary results that high-performing teams are capable of achieving. Create good team esteem by following these principles:

*I think if organizations are doing their job, then they create self-esteem in the workplace. The way a company works is because of the people. I think the attitude in the workplace completely dictates the quality of the product.*
**Nick Graham**

- Create a clear and compelling vision, mission, strategy, and challenging goals on which to focus. Establish clear priorities that minimize internal competition and turf conflicts.

- Clarify roles and responsibilities for all members that enable each to fully contribute his or her personal best to the team mission. Instill individuals with the obligation to act accountably toward one another and freely exercise the full range of their abilities to influence events and people.

- Foster an environment of inclusion and belonging in which teammates feel welcomed and accepted for who they are and what they bring to the team. Use diversity as a source of strength, not of tension and distrust.

- Support team members emotionally through thick and thin to demonstrate healthy caring for one another. Honor people's personal struggles.

- Maintain a balance between task performance and relationship effectiveness. Refuse to sacrifice working relationships to short-term business results. Respect process as the path to improving performance. People experience healthy and productive lives by balancing work and play.

- Create and maintain a feedback-rich environment in which people are expected and welcomed to freely give and receive feedback and coaching with teammates. Encourage appropriate risk-taking and learning behavior. Make it safe to fail (as long as the resulting learning is shared across the team).

- Insist that the team routinely invest time to celebrate and recognize its achievements and learnings. This nurtures pride, feelings of well-being, and a team image of high-performance capability. Such a team learns to deeply believe in itself and the abilities of its members.

Take a moment to assess your organization's use of these principles to help you to decide what you need to do to develop more team esteem.

**Our team has clear goals.**

| 1 | 2 | 3 | 4 | 5 |
|---|---|---|---|---|
| Never | Rarely | Frequently | Usually | Always |

**Team members know their roles and responsibilities.**

| 1 | 2 | 3 | 4 | 5 |
|---|---|---|---|---|
| Never | Rarely | Frequently | Usually | Always |

**Our team works in an environment of inclusion.**

| 1 | 2 | 3 | 4 | 5 |
|---|---|---|---|---|
| Never | Rarely | Frequently | Usually | Always |

**All team members support one another through thick and thin.**

| 1 | 2 | 3 | 4 | 5 |
|---|---|---|---|---|
| Never | Rarely | Frequently | Usually | Always |

**We maintain a balance between task performance and relationship building.**

| 1 | 2 | 3 | 4 | 5 |
|---|---|---|---|---|
| Never | Rarely | Frequently | Usually | Always |

**We nurture the development of a feedback-rich environment.**

| 1 | 2 | 3 | 4 | 5 |
|---|---|---|---|---|
| Never | Rarely | Frequently | Usually | Always |

**We remember to celebrate.**

| 1 | 2 | 3 | 4 | 5 |
|---|---|---|---|---|
| Never | Rarely | Frequently | Usually | Always |

With this assessment fresh in your mind, what are some of the key areas that your organization might need to work on first? Who could help you in addressing these issues? What steps might Forward the Action?

## Coping with Change and Loss: How Coaches Can Facilitate Healing

Most survivors of corporate America's restructuring activities go through an emotional adjustment period. People get hurt in organizational shake-ups. Deep feelings of loss resulting from what are extremely traumatic events often require time to heal. People need time to adjust to new bosses, locations, products, and teams. Most need time to fully understand their new roles and the new rules associated with the change. Coaches are in a position to facilitate healing.[15]

[15] A wonderful resource on healing is *Sensible Self-Help: The First Road Map for the Healing Journey* by Drs. David and Rebecca Grudermeyer and Lerissa Patrick. (Del Mar, CA: Willingness Works Press, 1995).

Much of the internal work that high performers do is with healing.[16] Almost invariably, high performers work on the principles described as The 7 H's of Healing: being here in the present, honesty, humility, honoring self and others, having a sense of humor, hope, and helpfulness.

## Being Here in the Present Moment

The human mind operates much like a pendulum. It swings to the *past*, where it accesses memory and all that it holds. It swings to the *future* and focuses on the potential that is not yet here. The precise bottom of the pendulum's cycle represents *here*, this present moment.

It is natural for our minds to work this way, but this emphasis on past and future sometimes is not helpful. It is not helpful to dwell on negative aspects of the past, such as regrets over mistakes made, resentments, and grudges against people whom we perceive have harmed us, judgments and negative attributions of motives, or the residue and "yuck" of unhealthy relationships.

It is more helpful, when recalling the past, to focus on our achievements (and those of other people), lessons we have learned, understandings we have developed, and the richness and personal growth of our unique histories. These thoughts correlate with higher thinking states such as curiosity, gratitude, and resourcefulness on the Mood Map (page 141).

When looking at the future, it is unhelpful to worry about what *might* happen,[17] to catastrophize (imagining the worst that could happen), or to fear change and the challenges that the future will bring. It is far more helpful to direct one's thoughts toward the positive aspects that change can create, the opportunity for renewal and a fresh start, the unforeseen beneficial possibilities just out of sight, and the very real hope for a better tomorrow.

Usually the human mind passes through the present moment very quickly, in small snippets. Typically, we spend far too little time focused on what or who is before us. To better capture the present moment, we must realize that the present moment is all

[16] The process described below is connected to the Mood Map (page 141). Work in these areas helps to elevate people into the higher states of mind and facilitates higher levels of functioning.

*In order to be utterly happy the only thing necessary is to refrain from comparing this moment with other moments in the past, which I often did not fully enjoy because I was comparing them with other moments of the future.*

**Andre Gide**

[17] Someone once defined worrying as "suffering in advance."

that we really have. The past is over and the future is not yet here. Right here, right now, is where our lives happen.

Transformational Coaches learn to manage their attention and focus their listening in the present moment. They learn to eliminate or minimize distractions and to effectively mitigate the effect of their communication filters. Have you ever been in a meeting physically but not emotionally? Have you seen others do the same? What is the outcome of the meeting if a large portion of the attendees are distracted by the past or future? Given the current stressful demands of our work, coaching others to stay focused becomes very relevant and helpful. Learning occurs and solutions present themselves in the here and now. All we have to do is to pay attention to what is before us.

## Honesty

We often vacillate between two extremes in our communications. At one end, we are indirect, afraid to speak up and tell the truth. At the other extreme, we can be so direct that we are brash and abrasive. Neither of these ends of the continuum is effective.

Honesty means having the awareness and courage to express your inside truth to the outside world. To be honest means to have integrity, to be authentic.

*Everybody talks about wanting to change things and help and fix, but ultimately all you can do is fix yourself. And that's a lot. Because if you can fix yourself, it has a ripple effect.*

**Rob Reiner**

The trouble is that many corporate environments make it unsafe to be totally truthful. Often well-intentioned leaders believe that they are better off with a spin on the facts; they interpret events and situations in the best light to maintain the corporate image. Although this practice may be appropriate in some situations, shading the truth is not a long-term successful strategy when it comes to people. People prefer to be treated as adults.

Transformational Coaches challenge themselves by:

- Checking their own intentions or purposes in all interactions

- Maintaining internal emotional integrity (doing frequent "gut" checks to be sure that things feel right)

- Refusing to lie to themselves or others

- Confronting the real issues in the workplace that affect people

- Offering feedback to those around them

- Learning how to constructively handle negative feelings such as anger, resentment, and emotional upset

## Humility

Humility is important in healing. Arrogance is the polar opposite of humility. Arrogant people usually are very difficult to work with because they always know the "right" answers. Arrogance parades as self-righteousness and condescending or judgmental behavior that alienates people.

Learning to live with humility means developing the ability to see ourselves in the actions of others. Other people become mirrors for us. We can learn to know that we *do not know* and to ask questions to find out. We can reject perfectionism as a disease of the soul and learn to accept ourselves and others with genuine positive regard.

Transformational Coaches:

- Realize their fallibility as human beings

- Learn to forgive themselves and others

- Embrace healthy curiosity as a lifelong learning stance

- Develop a practice of reflecting, praying, or meditating to deepen their appreciation for their lives and for the people in them

- See life as a journey and their choices as their unique paths

As a result, they become more compassionate with themselves, then they are able to offer that compassion to others.

## Honoring Self and Others

The antithesis of honor is judgment and lack of respect. To honor ourselves and others means to become compassionate and accepting of ourselves and our life experiences. We learn to develop *positive regard* for other people, the value they bring to us, and the organizations in which we work. We come to view our

*It is never too late to give up your prejudices.*
**Henry David Thoreau**

journeys through life and the work that we do as sacred, as containing a spiritual dimension.

Transformational Coaches ask effective questions and listen deeply to the responses. They listen more with their hearts than with their heads in order to honor the human experience. They drop positions and point-counterpoint arguments. They listen between the lines for the real messages.

### Having a Sense of Humor

When we stop taking things so seriously, we are able to see the lighter side of life. When we stop taking things so personally, we know that we are far more than our roles at work, our material possessions, or our achievements. We become detached from our outer images, the results that we create, and all the things that go on in our external worlds. We appreciate the folly of the human experience and are able to hold all of life more lightly.

*When people are not happy doing what they do, they don't do it as well as when they are happy.*

**Tom Landry**

Transformational Coaches realize the link between their thoughts and their realities and they learn to manage their thought processes. They realize that their work is too important to be taken seriously. They learn to see the humor in life and to share the funny things that happen all of the time, everywhere.

### Hope

We all know people whom we would describe as cynical or pessimistic. These people feel like black holes, sucking energy out of anybody who comes in contact with them.

An optimistic outlook on life accentuates the positive possibilities that could, can, and ought to be created. That is where a Transformational Coach places his or her energy for change. Effective leaders bring a positive yet realistic view of the future into clear focus when they articulate organizational vision and missions. Having hope includes adopting a long-term view.

The Transformational Coach learns the art of "possibility thinking" by focusing on a positive and compelling picture of the future. Holding a vision for the future that is brighter than today engenders commitment from people. Coaches capture people's hearts in the process of creating that future together. People learn to maintain a long-term and high-level perspective. They see things from a fresh viewing point with open, beginners' minds, as if they were seeing things for the first time.

### Helpfulness

Helpfulness has everything to do with intention. To be truly helpful means being able to set aside personal needs and to focus instead on the needs of others. The Transformational Coach learns that a service mindset is essential to coaching others. Helpfulness comes from the heart, not from the head. Therefore, Transformational Coaches practice a form of "tough love" in order to support and empower others to change rather than to enable them to stay stuck in ineffective behavior.

## Having a Real Effect

Working on the seven principles will allow you to develop the full potential of what it means to be human. As you learn to make amends (request forgiveness), let go of your need to control things and people, acknowledge your losses, and work on your own issues, you become more emotionally healthy. As you work on healing yourself, you become capable of facilitating healing in others. You cannot lead somebody where you have not yet journeyed.

The healing processes described above represent a lifetime's work for most of us. Unfortunately, there is no magic pill that will transform our lives overnight. Healing is less a destination than it is a journey. Through your own healing process, you can help other people see to themselves more clearly and to make healthier decisions about themselves in relation to their work, their relationships, and their lives. People who are able to live in states of curiosity, gratitude, and resourcefulness seem to have richer and more productive lives, and they create and contribute more to their teams and their organizations.

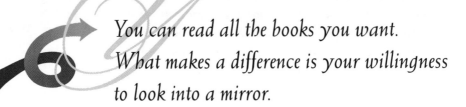

*You can read all the books you want.*
*What makes a difference is your willingness*
*to look into a mirror.*

DR. LAURA SCHLESHINGER

# Transformational Coaches Are Role Models

*Walking the Talk*

> *What you do speaks so loud that I cannot hear what you say.*
> **Ralph Waldo Emerson**

Role modeling derives its power from the psychological need for affiliation and approval. We need to fit in with the rest of our society, so we mimic the behavior of those around us, especially those who are obviously powerful.

When we are young and dependent on our parents or caretakers, they are, by default, our first role models. Later in life our teachers and other adults with whom we interact become our role models. In our work lives, our organization's leaders have the greatest effect on our behaviors. They become our role models for the world of work.

You probably have heard the phrase, "walking the talk." It is used to describe people whose actions are consistent with their spoken words. When leaders learn quickly to "talk the talk" but stop short of "walking the walk," they lose the credibility and trust that is essential to building a high-performance team. Many leaders are quick to enhance their vocabularies with the current buzz words of the program-of-the-month but are slower to align their behaviors to match.

Transformational Coaches learn to become aware of the significant effects of their personal behavior. They build integrity into their daily lives and encourage commitment from the people around them by acting out both their personal and the organization's values. Congruity is the key. The challenge is to live your message in all aspects of your being.

> *As I grow older, I pay less attention to what people say.*
> *I JUST WATCH WHAT THEY DO.*
> **Andrew Carnegie**

Every culture operates according to implicit and explicit values. It is important for coaches to reinforce the values of their organizations in all of their coaching behaviors and dialogues. People respect any coach who has the courage to follow his or her own convictions and advice. Conversely, people disrespect (and probably will not follow) the coach who says one thing and does another. Successful coaches *are* their messages.

> *The corporation can never be something we are not.*
> **Max DePree**

## Role Modeling Personal Growth

First and foremost, Transformational Coaches must role model openness and responsiveness to performance feedback from whatever source.

In *The One Minute Manager*, Ken Blanchard called feedback "the breakfast of champions"—an apt sports metaphor. Feedback is the primary way in which professional athletes learn about barriers that limit their performance. Most highly successful athletes hire not one, but several coaches, each with specialized training expertise and perspectives. They use their coaches' feedback to create a performance benchmark against which they monitor progress and change. Their coaches make the difference between their success and failure. From athletes, we can learn to love feedback as a way of growing and developing to our full potential.

## Role Modeling Self-Disclosure

If coaches intend to lead others by example, the example must include self-disclosure. Self-disclosure promotes an emotionally safe environment which is necessary to support a feedback-rich, high-performance culture. The coaches disclose appropriate things about themselves that other, less courageous leaders would not. They speak the unspeakable—they name their assumptions, their judgments, their fears, their agendas, and their beliefs. They share their experiences and they invite their coachees to do the same.[19]

You can do this, too. First, share with others more of what makes you tick. What are your thoughts and feelings about what is actually happening in the company? If you are less protective and more open, vulnerable, and honest, you will begin to change the tone of communications from cautious protectionism to openness. Respectfully delivered, honest communications build trust.

Share more of your feelings about your work, including your hopes, joys, fears, and frustrations. This "feeling" content may make you more human and easier to connect with. Even riskier, on a personal basis, would be sharing what you are working on to improve your personal effectiveness. What are you learning about yourself from your feedback? What goals do you have to grow and develop professionally and as a human being? Obviously, use judgment in selecting the people with whom you share.

Second, ask for feedback. We all have blind spots in our attitudes, behaviors, and actions. We are not able to perceive clearly how we affect others in the various roles we play in our organizations. This information, if we could receive it with the right attitudes, could be immensely valuable in helping us to understand how to make positive changes in the ways in which we interact with others.

Asking for feedback is one of the most powerful actions you can take as a coach. Earnestly communicate your own desire to

[19] The Johari window is an extremely helpful framework by which to explore the unknown. Its power is to help people explore ways to expand the visibility of the private self so that others are able to see and thus appreciate more of who they are.

learn and grow as a person, as a professional, and as a coach. Let people know that you cannot do that in a vacuum. You need their feedback. Ask questions of your teammates that are personal and that promote learning. "Questions to Promote Feedback," which follow, can serve as inspiration.

On a more structured basis, 360° feedback processes promote deep individual and team learning, especially when they are focused on the organization's core values and guiding behaviors.[18] I have helped many leaders interpret their feedback and create potent and responsive action plans to address the issues raised. The powerful role modeling this demonstrates cannot be overstated.

[18] 360° feedback processes have become a very popular way of gathering feedback from one's boss, peers, and direct reports.

**Questions To Promote Feedback**

## Questions by the Coach

**Questions Leading to Reinforcement:**
What am I doing that you find helpful?
What behaviors should I keep doing?
What are improvements you have seen me make?
What aspects of my leadership/coaching are becoming better?

**Questions Leading to Learning:**
What behaviors might be unclear or confusing?
Do I send mixed signals to you or the team?
Do you believe that I am on the right track?

**Questions Leading to Change:**
What behaviors seem counterproductive or out-of-phase?
What suggestions would you like me to consider?
What behaviors could I consider stopping or starting?

**Reflective Questions for the Coach:**
Am I listening and responding to feedback regarding my leadership effectiveness?
Am I becoming less effective, more effective, or maintaining the status quo?
Am I initiating informal requests for feedback on my effectiveness as a coach?
What does this feedback indicate for my coaching effectiveness?
What am I learning about the coaching process (what's easy or challenging)?
What are the key themes suggested by the feedback?
What improvement steps might I take to enhance my coaching effectiveness?
Where am I stuck and what support do I need to improve?
How am I sharing what I'm learning about coaching with other members of my team?

# PART THREE

# Creating a High-Performance Coaching Culture

THE FIRST TWO PARTS of this book have defined, illustrated, and personalized the process of coaching. This section will address the application of Transformational Coaching throughout the organization for the purpose of creating high performance in individuals, teams, and organizations. It starts with a vision of what a coaching culture looks like.

❧

*Men and women want to do a good job,*
*and if they are provided the proper environment,*
*they will do so.*
**Bill Hewlett**

*Real education consists of drawing the best out of yourself.*

MAHATMA MOHANDAS GHANDI

# The Vision of High Performance

## The High-Performance Paradigm

Organizations that consistently achieve high performance are supported by high-performance cultures. Certain characteristics distinguish these cultures.

## Traits of a High-Performance Culture

The traits of a high-performance culture can be synthesized into what I call *The Seven C's of High-Performance Teams*. They are:

- They are on a *clear course*. Everyone knows in what direction the organization is moving and everyone is purposefully moving in the same direction

- Team members demonstrate a high sense of *commitment* to the organization, the team, and one another

- *Communications* among the team members are extremely effective in promoting learning and focused on Forwarding the Action

- The *character* of the organization is defined by members' behaviors being congruent with the organization's stated shared values

- The organization—and the individuals in it—are open to and comfortable with *change*. The organization anticipates, responds, and adapts creatively when changes are desired

- There is a spirit of *collaboration* among the organization's members, as the operative way of interacting in functional and cross-functional teams

- *Coaching* is practiced up, down, and across the organization

The figure on the next page shows the Seven C's of High-Performance Teams, and the following paragraphs describe each of the seven traits in detail.

## Course

If the course is sufficiently clear and supported, it provides context for and guides the team's actions. A clear course is a necessary condition for strategic success. A clear course is composed of:

- A clear purpose, vision, mission, strategy, goals, priorities, and action plans to move the business forward. These components define the directional system for the business—a sort of internal gyroscope

- Goals and objectives that are clear, specific, achievable, challenging, measurable, current, understood by all, and well coordinated to minimize internal competition

- A clear sense of the key strategic priorities of the business and how they change over time

- Performance measurement and reporting systems that are effective in clearly indicating success or failure in achieving the goals

## The Seven C's of High-Performance Teams

This illustration provides a clear "high-performance paradigm" of the strategic competencies that are necessary to create a significant competitive advantage for organizations and teams. Performance can be systematically assessed against the core curriculum for each dimension and a process designed to develop the missing or underdeveloped competencies that are required to produce a feedback-rich, team-based, high-performance environment.

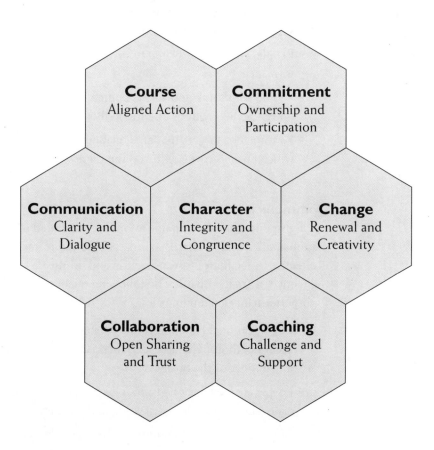

## Commitment

Commitment is the unwavering choice to support the team and the team's objectives with one's best personal efforts. This quality establishes the necessary conditions for individual and team excellence. High performance requires clear roles, responsibilities, accountabilities, and the explicit individual and group agreements that empower people to risk action in the face of uncertainty. The characteristics of high commitment include the following:

- People who are committed to the clear roles and responsibilities of all team members, which are properly aligned to support the business direction

- People who are motivated to give their best personal performance

- People who think and act accountably, taking full responsibility for their actions and the results they create

- Performance targets that are collaboratively established, which ensures ownership and the highest levels of participation

## Communications

High-performance communications are facilitated when information and learning is shared among people and teams. When it is effective, it facilitates forward action and positive results; if ineffective, it creates chaos. The following qualities describe high-performance communication:

- Organizational communications are consistent, timely, accurate, thorough, clear, and focused on the strategic imperatives of the business

- People are well informed about external market issues, especially about customer satisfaction and competitive threats

- Organizational communications help people to complete their jobs more effectively and perform better in their roles

- Interpersonal communications are characterized as respectful and healthy and serve to build trust and connection across teams

## Character

Character refers to the defining qualities and values of the team which guide decisions concerning internal and external constituencies of the organization. The values and behaviors modeled by leadership establish the tone and expectations for the entire organization, making it a place in which people feel proud to work.

*Some say knowledge is power, but that is not true. Character is power.*
**Sathya Sai Baba**

High character includes the following:

- The organization is guided by clearly articulated values and guiding behaviors that establish an internal code of conduct for behavior and a framework for business decisions

- All levels of the organization understand, appreciate, and demonstrate their commitment to the values through their congruent behavior

- Standards of high integrity and ethics guide all daily activities and long-term strategic decisions

- The organization does the right thing for its employees, treating them with utmost respect, compassion, and fairness

## Change

Change is the process through which people and organizations continuously enhance their effectiveness. As John Kotter and James Heskett (1992) note (see Chapter 1), the adaptability of an organization determines how well it weathers changes in the business environment. The business case for change outlines the big picture; continuous-improvement processes provide process-improvement technologies to improve systems; and Transformational Coaching provides the empathy to support people during the emotional process of letting go.

Savvy leaders follow an enlightened approach to leading change by directly addressing the issues that create fear, resistance, and sabotage of the change initiative. This process stimulates creativity and innovation, and resistance evaporates. Key characteristics for high-performing teams include:

- The team quickly adapts to the changing external environment by changing internal processes and systems

- People who are affected by change are highly involved in its creation and implementation

- People are supported in being innovative and creative in solving business problems and taking appropriate levels of risk

- People are encouraged to learn from their mistakes and share their learning across the team

### Collaboration

Teamwork in a high-performance organization is demonstrated by people's willingness to form partnerships beyond simple "win/win" outcomes to create synergistic gains for the business. Internal politics, competition, and conflict inhibit the open sharing of breakthrough ideas which are needed to solve difficult business problems. Beyond common goals, skills for conflict resolution, trust building, and effective decision making are needed to create the optimal environment of mutual support. Characteristics of collaboration include:

- Teams openly support other teams and functions in working on common goals

- Turf battles and conflicts across functions are resolved quickly into "win/win" solutions

- People frequently and openly discuss and resolve issues that interfere with organizational performance

- Consensus decision-making models build participation and enhance trust throughout the organization

### Coaching

Transformational Coaching is the art of empowering people to improve their effectiveness, in a way in which they feel helped. This process engages the huge untapped potential within people and organizations by focusing energy on key performance objectives. Coaching, as a key component of leadership, brings out the

best in people. Characteristics of high-performance teams
include:

- Leaders and managers become excellent performance
  coaches, role modeling both giving and receiving performance feedback

- The culture becomes "feedback-rich," as teammates at all
  levels provide performance feedback in all directions

- Performance feedback is delivered on an ongoing basis
  and is not saved up for year-end performance appraisals

- People eagerly anticipate opportunities to be coached
  because the process helps them to develop personally and
  professionally

All of the characteristics described above create and are supported by a "feedback-rich" environment.

## The Feedback-Rich Environment

High-performance teams accomplish things better, faster, and
more simply than non-high-performance teams. Their communication processes create and nurture a feedback-rich environment.
The members of these teams invest time in developing and maintaining the quality of intragroup and intergroup communications
to achieve the highest levels of performance. The following characteristics both describe and facilitate the development of the
feedback-rich environment that is required to create and sustain
high performance.

- Mutual accountability
- Willingness to learn
- No fear
- No surprises
- Truthfulness
- Self-responsible language
- Coaching

### Mutual Accountability

In a feedback-rich environment, team members accept 100 percent responsibility for the outcomes of their communications. You might think that 50/50 would be fair, but look at it this way: If each person in a partnership assumes 50 percent of the responsibility for the outcomes of their joint communications, each can always blame the other for failures, claiming that "I kept my end of the agreement, but you didn't."

Alternatively, if both parties agree that each is fully accountable for the results of their communications, it sets up a condition of no blame, no excuses, no hiding, and no victims. Each takes responsibility to clear up misunderstandings and emotional residue that could build up between them. Each commits to creating and maintaining a squeaky-clean relationship in which thoughts, feelings, and experiences are quickly shared. This minimizes complications downstream and keeps the feedback flowing.

### Willingness To Learn

Learning is an orientation and a mindset. People who are willing to learn facilitate the expression of new ideas, including those that are "off the wall." In a feedback-rich environment, everyone seeks fresh input continually, to expand the thinking processes and the knowledge base on which decisions are made. The culture emphasizes ongoing personal, professional, and technical developments that support the capability of the team to expand its performance. Frequent, frank, and fair debriefs focused on sharing the lessons learned are the norm.

### No Fear

Fear inhibits the flow of feedback. When messengers are shot for delivering bad news, the emperor insists that everyone admire his new clothes, and all the cows are sacred, the environment breeds fear and distrust. In this artificial, emotionally unsafe environment, people will fear the consequences of making even an occasional mistake (regardless of whether they learn from it). They do not offer feedback because they fear reprisal, especially when the receiver of the feedback is The Boss.

The prerequisite for a feedback-rich environment is emotional safety—room for people to honestly (and without fear of the consequences) express their thoughts, feelings, and opinions; deliver performance feedback as easily upward as downward; and challenge conventions and traditions.

## No Surprises

It takes continual ongoing communication to eliminate the surprises that frequently derail individual or team performance. Communications need to be explicit and frequent, focused on continually updating status, progress, and obstacles to achieving goals. In this environment, the baton is not dropped as it is passed between players. People take accountability for keeping the information flowing and for not allowing "black holes" (where information disappears) to develop. People are comfortable in examining trends (positive or negative) and they rely on and express their intuition. Early warning is the operative approach that builds trust levels.

## Truthfulness

When people tell intellectual and emotional truths, others trust them implicitly. A high-performance team values honesty and encourages team members to share their thoughts and feelings in order to develop trust across the team and to make better business decisions. Issues are confronted constructively and quickly, with full disclosure of all agendas, needs, and wants. People choose not to waste energy by posturing, manipulating, and doctoring communication. The net result across the team is that the messages are trusted and do not have to be filtered.

## Self-Responsible Language

In a feedback-rich environment, people express their points of view from the "I" perspective. Feedback is, therefore, highly owned by the individuals who express it. People do not attempt to speak for others, only for themselves. This keeps communication very clean and clear. The word "we" is not used very much either, unless all parties in the *we* are present. Again, high-performance teams are clear.

Similarly, the word "they" is rarely used. *They* so easily become the enemy because, first of all, *we* do not know who *they* are, and second, we do not know if *they* said it. "They" is confusing and unclear.

Self-responsible behavior includes confronting counterproductive gossip. Somewhat paradoxically, high-performance teams with feedback-rich environments rely on the informal communication system (the grapevine) to enhance the overall connectivity of the organization. In these cultures, the formal and informal communication systems synchronistically coexist and mutually support performance improvement across the organization. Both systems tend to carry the same information.

### Coaching

A feedback-rich environment relies on coaching as the requisite communication skill of all members of that high-performance culture. Transformational Coaching flows freely among teammates, teams, and functions. Coaching occurs in a 360° fashion, up, down, and all across the team. Every person in a leadership role is committed to mastering coaching. Customer feedback is always sought and responded to and becomes one of the driving forces for strategic change.

# Creating a High-Performance Organization

*Implementing Corporate Culture Change*

Cultural change must be crafted to touch the hearts and minds of people. It is less a matter of managing than it is a matter of leading. As a successful cultural-change initiative unfolds, it should be obvious to every member of the culture that leaders embrace the change. Senior leadership must share full accountability for the success of the initiative, even if the change effort includes the use of outside consultants.

Do not underestimate the challenge of creating a cultural shift. Human organizations build up tremendous inertia over time, and it takes tremendous initiative and determination to budge them. Imagine a fully loaded oil tanker steaming ahead at 30 knots. It takes *miles* of ocean and massive amounts of force for it to change direction substantially. It takes similar amounts of energy for people to change their beliefs, habits, thinking, and rationale for how things always have been done. Such changes require a long-term commitment and sustained application of time and energy from the leadership and the organization.

It is also critical that the cultural-change process be viewed as an ongoing process, not as a project with an end point. Senior

*The moment we break faith with one another, the sea engulfs us and the light goes out.*
**James Baldwin**

leaders should be directly supported with a personal executive coach for at least the first year of the change process so that they can sustain their commitment and effectiveness in role modeling the new cultural behaviors. If they do not change, the culture will not change.

## The Challenge

Creating high performance requires the strategy, structure, and culture of the organization to be in alignment. Having these major components out of sync creates interference. With high levels of alignment, the strategic direction of the business is the primary organizing principle for the supporting organizational structure and the operative culture.

"Culture" is loosely defined as "how we do things around here." It consists of attitudes, beliefs, and behaviors that both describe and guide the ways in which people interact. When business leaders talk about cultural alignment, they mean how well the organizational culture fits the current strategy of the business.

For a classic illustration of how alignment affects performance, look at the telecommunications industry. Before deregulation, AT&T's organizing principle was "Universal service, anywhere in the country." To make this a reality, AT&T created a huge bureaucratic organization resembling an army steeped in uniform procedures and systems. Efficiency was important, especially to support extraordinary emergency actions in the face of disasters.

Culturally, it was not important to be creative. It was, however, critical to follow the chain of command. Costs of operation were allowed to be passed on to customers. After all, it was a monopoly.

With deregulation in the early 1980s, the industry was turned upside down.

Initially, the regional telephone companies (the "baby Bells") still had protected territories, but with ongoing deregulation, cable companies, television stations, and entertainment giants have entered the field. Now, the telephone companies' organizational structures need to be lean, nimble, and focused on serving customers. Culturally, teamwork, creativity, openness to change, and a sense of urgency have become important strategic values, because more nimble, entrepreneurial skills are needed to face the competitive threats.

For an organization to be successful in a changing world, the culture must adapt to the push and pull of the customer and the changing competitive landscape. Feedback from the marketplace regarding customers and competitors is a vital information link— so vital, in fact, that it must be the organizing principle.

To assess how well aligned your culture is with the realities of the marketplace, answer the following questions.

Does your culture:

- Focus on the common purpose of serving the customer?

- Foster aligned action, collaboration, and support across the business?

- Energize people's creative problem-solving talents?

- Stress a balance between efficiency and effectiveness?

- Encourage learning to create a competitive advantage for the business?

- Create a mindset of accountability and reward performance?

- Enhance people's commitment and mutual trust with open dialogue?

- Nurture a set of shared values as the "glue" for teams?

The next section describes the principles of creating the culture that enables an organization to become and remain high-performance.

## The Seven Principles of Cultural Change

There are seven distinct, interdependent, synergistic, and compulsory principles that make cultural change possible. Without them, it is impossible. The seven principles are:

1. Educate to the need
2. Define the new culture
3. Align to it
4. Build skills and solve problems
5. Communicate continuously
6. Systematize
7. Coach to it

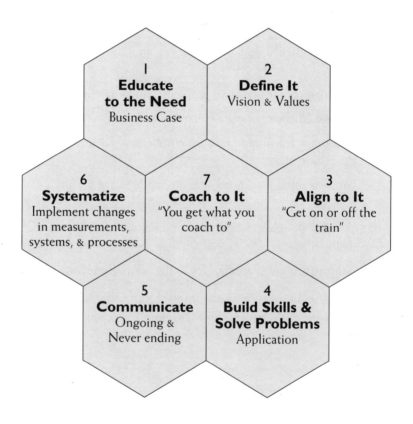

## Principle 1: Educate to the Need

The first step in cultural change is educating the members of the culture about why changes are necessary. Because leaders set the tone, pace, and expectations for performance, education begins with the senior leadership team and focuses on developing the case for change. Change is more effective—and only will be sustained—when leaders are its champions. The case for change defines the business imperative with a sense of urgency to stimulate immediate, enterprise-wide action.

During the educational phase, information is gathered about the current culture's key strengths and challenges. After analyzing this information, leadership can determine the culture's ability to support its long-term business goals. The data help to shape a change strategy to accomplish the objectives. In addition, this fact-finding and learning process will help create among the senior leadership team a shared understanding of what needs to be done and why.

## Principle 2: Define the New Culture

The leaders articulate or update the organization's purpose, vision, mission, and strategy documents. They answer the questions, "Who are we?," "Who are our customers?," "Where are we going?," and "What steps will take us there?" They need to accomplish this task collaboratively in order to create a high level of ownership and to set the conditions for alignment across the leadership team. This means that, as the culture-shaping process unfolds, other members of the culture must have an opportunity to provide input. Processes follow to ensure that result.

Equally important is a shared set of core values—behavioral guides that explicitly define expectations of everyone in the organization. It is crucial that these values be comprehensive, appropriate for the business environment, and 100 percent supported by leadership. These values are fully aligned to support the business strategy.

### Principle 3: Align to It

Alignment is not a matter of adopting new slogans and buzz-words. You can not lead an organization by only "talking the talk." You must walk it every day or else it is a sham. People see right through it. In addition, fractionalized or self-serving leadership—leaders who seek to fulfill their own agendas—zaps organizational spirit and performance.

*Trust is the lubrication that makes it possible for organizations to work.*

**Warren Bennis
and Burt Nanus**

To be credible to the rest of the organization, the values and guiding behaviors articulated during the definition process must be genuinely embraced by the leadership team. So long as there is a high level of congruency between what leaders say and what leaders do, trust blooms. Lack of trust creates huge interference, which inhibits high performance and stalls the cultural shift.

A 360° feedback process is an extremely powerful alignment tool when it is used to provide feedback about alignment with organizational values. It also produces a rich database that can serve the ongoing development of executive leadership through an executive-coaching process.

## General Electric's Leadership Alignment Model

**Living the Values**

Coach to
improve performance

**Aligned &
High-Performance
Team Player**

Support, promote, and
enroll as a Coach

**Attitude, Style &
Performance Difficulties**

Wrong person
for this company

**Achieving Results**

Coach to align on values

Commitment

VALUES AND BEHAVIORS ▲

Lip Service

**Living
the
Values**

Poor Performance    RESULTS AND PERFORMANCE ▶    High Performance

## Contributing to the Business

During the alignment process—and after a reasonable adjustment period with ample coaching—those who are not willing or able to align their attitudes and actions with the new direction and focus of the culture should be released to other endeavors. Energy drains on the enterprise simply cannot be tolerated.

Successful organizations have started to use values-based hiring profiles to help find people who "fit" their organizations. Years ago, Jack Welsh of General Electric instituted a practice whereby people are evaluated not only on their objective performance but also on the degree to which their behaviors reflect the values that are in "alignment" with GE's. People whose values are "out of phase" are coached and, even if their job performance is great, if they do not adjust to "living the values," they are asked to go elsewhere. GE's Leadership Alignment model, at left, graphically illustrates this concept. GE's application of the principle of "finding the right fit" is important for coaches. High performance hangs in the balance.

### Principle 4: Build Skills and Solve Problems

During this part of the culture-strengthening process, team workshops are used to build new attitudes and skills and to make sure that workshop participants apply their new skills to create solutions for strategic issues already defined. Energy and momentum are added to the change process when people see immediate results from their efforts; commitment is built when problems are solved by working together in the change process.

The most important collaborative skills are:

- Strategic thinking
- Planning and prioritizing
- Leading and supporting change, creativity, and innovation
- Interpersonal and organizational communication
- Fostering commitment
- Transformational Coaching
- Continuous-improvement processes

It is in this step that people learn Transformational Coaching skills.

During these team workshops, formal, written agreements can be used effectively to create a strong bond of mutual commitment and to provide clear guidance and support for the journey that lies ahead. Team agreements capture the behavioral components of working together in the new culture. Individual leadership contracts help all team members to focus on appropriately responding to their feedback in order to enhance their overall effectiveness.

### Principle 5: Communicate Continuously

A feedback-rich, high-performance environment is possible only in an organization in which cultural values and expectations set the standard for continual communication. From the very beginning of the cultural-change initiative, the organization must be informed of the business case for change, the change process envisioned, and the ongoing progress made toward the objectives of this initiative. The rationale contained in the business case for change must reach the entire organization, so that everybody understands the necessity of the change process.

It is critical that ongoing performance and process improvements and individual and team commitments be broadcast across the organization in order to acknowledge and reinforce their effect. As a guideline, all business communications should contain some cultural message or update. At least 20 percent of communications should be focused on the culture and no more than 80 percent should be focused on the business. This keeps the change message alive and in front of people.

### Principle 6: Systematize

Ignore this phase and you will fail. This sixth principle gives the cultural-change initiative the teeth it needs to be taken seriously.

Systematization means aligning all the processes and systems within the organization to the vision and values of the change effort. Make and reinforce clear links among vision, mission, strategy, and goals and other concurrent organizational initiatives, such as continuous improvement, total quality, process re-engineering, customer service, market growth, and/or new-product development.

Any system or process that touches people, such as hiring, training, promoting, rewarding, reassigning and releasing, needs to be aligned with the values and guiding behaviors that define the new strategy and culture. The trick is that these efforts must be executed *while the other phases are under construction*. It is a little like passengers redesigning and reconstructing an airplane while in flight.

### Principle 7: Coach to It

Coaching is absolutely critical to this change process. Wise management practice has always been that performance follows what we pay attention to. In other words, we get what we coach to. Coaching activates the power of the self-fulfilling prophecy. If goals and outcomes are clearly stated, and the measurement and reward systems support those goals, organizational transformation can occur.

Coaching helps people to connect to whatever leadership defines, measures, and rewards. Coaching connects:

- People to people—to form trusting relationships
- People to processes—for continuous improvement
- People to performance—to focus on creating sustainable results
- Processes to performance—to create more results

The following paragraphs describe these connections in greater detail.

#### CONNECTING PEOPLE TO PEOPLE

As people enter into a coaching relationship, they learn new things about one another, including likes, dislikes, preferences, personal values, career objectives, and personal and professional frustrations. The coaching journey is truly a process of mutual discovery through which deeper levels of trust, respect, and appreciation can develop. It is through Transformational Coaching dialogue that people learn how to work together more effectively and use the coaching process to leverage enhanced results.

*A culture is defined by how well its people connect.*
**MCI television commercial, 1997**

### CONNECTING PEOPLE TO PROCESSES

The Transformational Coaching process can be used to effectively focus people's attention on the continuous-improvement processes that lead to positive change, innovation, and renewal.

Process improvement and continuous improvement lead to enhanced ways of meeting the challenges of the business. It starts with seeing the advantages and benefits of examining "the way we've always done it" and discovering better, faster, and simpler ways of satisfying customers' needs. This also includes developing a full range of quality-improvement tools to systematically capture improvement opportunities.

### CONNECTING PEOPLE TO PERFORMANCE

Connecting people to their accomplishments is another primary objective of Transformational Coaching. It is an irony that our results-obsessed Western culture generally does a poor job of acknowledging people for their contributions. Modern corporations, while evolving out of the Industrial-Age mentality and its Theory-X management philosophy, still tend to view people as interchangeable and replaceable parts of the profit machinery. Too often, managers take people for granted and fail to deliver genuine appreciation and acknowledgment for the part they play in accomplishing the objectives of the organization. A Transformational Coach realizes that performance is enhanced when people develop genuine pride in themselves, their teams, and their organizations.

*The best way to cheer yourself up is to cheer everybody else up.*
**Samuel Longhorn Clemens (Mark Twain)**

### CONNECTING PROCESSES TO PERFORMANCE

The coaching process helps people to connect the performance objectives of their teams with the business processes used to attain them. Western business mentality tends to discount process in favor of results. The total-quality movement and process re-engineering have taught us that improving processes enhances performance. Process holds the key; coaching can help make that connection crystal clear.

⚜

*The people, led by wise leadership, will come to the realization,*
*"We did it ourselves."*

**Lao-Tsu**

*Every man must decide whether he will walk in the light of*
*creative altruism or the darkness of destructive selfishness.*
*This is the judgment.*
*Life's most persistent and urgent question is,*
*What are you doing for others?*

**MARTIN LUTHER KING, JR.**

# Coaching Is a Journey

The process of becoming a coach is not a destination. It is a journey—a path without an end. You will never arrive. I have not. My experience has been that the more coaching I do, the more proficient I become, the more people I touch, the more I realize that there is more to be done and more to learn.

Coaching requires the very best from all aspects of our humanity. It is not a path for the weak-hearted or for people who are afraid to grow. It is a path for the courageous and for people who are committed to making a difference in the lives of those they touch through coaching.

In many ways, Transformational Coaching is about treating others the way you want to be treated. The message is simple, profound, and expressed in all of the major religions of the world. It seems universally important to display the compassion that permits rapport and connection to others.[20]

**Christianity**: Do unto others as you would have them do unto you.

**Hinduism**: Do naught to others which, if done to thee, would cause thee pain; this is the sum of duty.

[20] *Chop Wood, Carry Water* by Rick Fields (New York: Jeremy P. Tarcher, 1984).

**Buddhism**: A clansman [should] minister to his friends and familiars…by treating them as he treats himself.

**Confucianism**: The Master replied: "…what you do not want done to yourself, do not do unto others."

**Taoism**: To those who are good to me, I am good; and to those who are not good to me, I am also good. And thus all get to be good.

**Zorastrianism**: Whatever thou dost not approve for thyself, do not approve for anyone else. When thou hast acted in this manner, thou art righteous.

**Judaism**: Take heed to thyself, my child, in all thy works; and be discreet in all thy behavior. And what thou thyself hatest, do to no man.

**Greek Philosophy**: Do not do to others what you would not wish to suffer yourself; treat your friends as you would want them to treat you.

There is probably nothing in this book that you have not heard before. *The Heart of Coaching* is, I hope, full of common-sense teachings that are familiar to us all. The power we all possess is not in dreaming or envisioning wondrous, exciting new things to think and to say in order to impress others. Rather, it is more like the monk who was asked what his life was like *before* he became enlightened. He replied, "I chopped wood and carried water." When asked what it was like *after* enlightenment, he responded, "I chop wood and carry water." It is not *what* we do that changes, it is *how* we do it and *the fact that* we do it.

Self-empowerment is taking action on what you already know; it is feeling the fear and doing it anyway; it is not waiting for permission to do what you know in your heart is the right thing to do. You are already a coach. Otherwise you would not have read this book.

Now, go do what you know needs to be done.

⚹

*People are unreasonable, illogical, self-centered.*
**Love them anyway.**

*If you do good, people will accuse you of selfish, ulterior motives.*
**Do good anyway.**

*If you are successful, you will win false friends and true enemies.*
**Try to be successful anyway.**

*The good you do today will be forgotten tomorrow.*
**Do it anyway.**

*Honesty and frankness make you vulnerable.*
**Be honest and frank anyway.**

*What you spend years building may be destroyed overnight.*
**Build anyway.**

*People really need help, but they may attack you if you help them.*
**Help them anyway.**

*Give the world the best you have, and you'll get kicked in the teeth.*
**Give the world the best you have anyway.**

**Karl Menninger**

# Preparation for a Transformational Coaching Session

Coachee: _____ Date: _____ Time: _____

## Preparation

Observation: _____

Purpose of session: _____

## Learning Loop

Feedback: _____

Result/outcome/impact (Performance & people): _____

Question(s) to ask: _____

_____

Personal experience to share: _____

## Forwarding-the-Action

Positives to reinforce: _____

Possibilities to suggest: _____

_____

Specific behaviors to request: _____

Behaviors required and clear consequences: _____

_____

Action commitment: _____

Support offered: _____

# Sources for "Contrasting the Generations"

The following sources were used in compiling the table "Contrasting the Generations" on page 153.

*Fortune*, October 4, 1993, "Why Busters Hate Boomers"
*Newsweek*, June 6, 1994, "The Luck of the X'ers" By Jane Bryant Quinn
*Training*, May, 1994, "More Light on Generation X—The Psychological Contract"
*Training*, April, 1994, "It's Just a Job" by Bob Filipczak
*HR Magazine*, May, 1994, "The X Generation" by Kim Macalister

## About the Author

Thomas G. Crane is a consultant, facilitator, and coach who specializes in coaching leaders to build high-performance teams. He works with leaders and leadership teams to enhance individual leadership effectiveness so that people can better lead their organizations toward performance objectives.

For over a decade, he has refined his techniques as a consultant and engagement leader navigating strategic change and cultural alignment in large and small organizations. Organizations with whom he has worked include:

| | | | |
|---|---|---|---|
| AES Corporation | Continental Airlines | Holiday Inn Select | San Diego State University |
| Anadarko Petroleum | Crowne Plaza Hotels | Home Savings of America | Shell Oil Company |
| Corporation | Dixieline | Host Travel Division— | Southern California Gas |
| A.T. Kearney | Duty Free International | Marriott | Southern Natural Gas |
| Baker & Botts | ENRON Corp. | KFC | Teledyne Ryan Aeronautical |
| Bell Atlantic | Florida Power & Light | KPMG Peat Marwick | Transco Energy |
| E.F. Brady & Associates | GPU Nuclear | Los Alamos Laboratory | United Airlines |
| CBS | Helen Woodward Animal | NY Life | Vastar Resources |
| Concepts Meeting and Trade | Center | Nth Generation Computing | Von's Grocery Company |
| Show Management, Inc. | Hilton Grand Vacations | NYNEX | Westrend Electric, Inc. |

His company, Crane Consulting, focuses on helping leaders create the feedback-rich, team-based, high-performance organizations described in this book by providing:

- **360° feedback instruments** such as The 7 C's of Transformational Coaching (see below), The 7 C's of High-Performing Teams, and other instruments to assess the critical competencies required for increased performance
- **Organizational assessments and surveys** designed to understand the strategic and cultural issues that inhibit high-performance
- **Senior leadership team-building** sessions and retreats designed to create ownership and alignment around a common vision, mission, and values
- **Middle management sessions** designed to create optimum commitment and enrollment in the process of change
- **Executive coaching** to assist leaders and managers in courageously acting on what they know will enhance their personal and interpersonal effectiveness
- **Strategic planning retreats** to formulate business strategy, action plans, and priorities
- **Meeting facilitation and feedback** to enhance group dynamics in support of cultural transformation

# Crane Consulting's Transformational Coaching Workshops

The **7 C's of Transformational Coaching** is a competency-based 360° feedback model that serves as the basis for custom-designed workshops for leaders, managers, and supervisors. It is one of the first 360's to focus exclusively on the specific coaching competencies required for people to effectively motivate today's workforce.

The 7 C's are:

### Clear
It is essential that the communication process through which the coaching is delivered is effective at creating a shared understanding. The Transformational Coach consciously eliminates ambiguity and mixed messages. The coach pays attention to how the message is interpreted by the coachee and uses active listening skills to insure understanding.

### Committed
The Transformational Coach's commitment to the coachee's success is the foundation for trust and rapport in the relationship. This helps the coachee to build personal confidence in the security of the coaching relationship and creates a safe environment for risk taking.

### Courageous
The Transformational Coach must act with courage in the face of interpersonal or organizational challenges. Being open and vulnerable is part of what it takes to establish and maintain trust. Coaching requires the skillful confrontation of issues that may be uncomfortable to address. Facing issues head-on is an accountable behavior that moves people and the organization forward.

### Challenging
A Transformational Coach's purpose is to bring out the best in people. This is accomplished by looking for positive ways to stretch and develop others. The coach encourages people to develop new skills outside of their personal zone of comfort by constructively challenging the coachee's thinking, attitudes, beliefs, and behaviors.

**Collaborative**

The Transformational Coach works to create a partnership that "levels the playing field" with the coachee. Though the coach and coachee have different roles in the organization, the coach nurtures an egalitarian, high-trust, partnering relationship that transforms the way they work together. This sets the condition for dramatic performance improvements.

**Compassionate**

Fear inhibits people from performing up to their potential. As the Transformational Coach brings acceptance and forgiveness, while allowing a reasonable freedom to fail, a safe environment is created that supports learning, appropriate experimentation, and growth in people.

**Congruent**

People pay more attention to what others do—and less to what they say. If there is perceived disparity, trust is lost. The Transformational Coach must be aligned in thoughts, words, and actions to be a positive model of the attitudes and behaviors valued by the organization.

Clients have found these workshops and this 360° feedback process to be a powerful way of developing leadership effectiveness across their organizations.

Please call to discuss how we might integrate this workshop into your portfolio of leadership and management development programs.

Prior to founding Crane Consulting, Tom was a vice president of Senn-Delaney Leadership Consulting Group. In addition, he has worked in financial planning and project management roles with Solar Turbines, a division of Caterpillar. He currently is a member of the San Diego chapters of the Organization Development Network, the American Society for Training and Development, and the Society for Human Resource Management.

Tom lives in San Diego with his wife, Maggie, who is a partner in the business and a professional speaker on coaching, leadership, stress management, and other life effectiveness skills. They can be reached at:

 **CRANE CONSULTING**

11052 Picaza Place
San Diego, CA 92127
619/487-9017
Fax 619/592-0689

tgcrane@craneconsulting.com
www.craneconsulting.com

# Request for Feedback

I hope that you've found *The Heart of Coaching* helpful and enjoyable. In the spirit of coaching, I'd like your feedback. Please feel free to use your own format.

1. What I like most about this book is:


2. What I like least about this book is:


3. My specific suggestions for improving the book are:


4. Other comments:


**Optional:**

Date: _____

Your name: _____

Occupation: _____

May I reprint your comments, either in promotional material for *The Heart of Coaching* or in future
   publications? ☐ Yes ☐ No

If Yes, may I use your name? ☐ Yes ☐ No

If Yes, please provide your address and a daytime phone number so that I may contact you:

Address: _____

Phone: (_____)_____

Thank you!

   Thomas G. Crane
   Crane Consulting

11052 Picaza Place • San Diego, CA 92127 • 619/487-9017 • Fax 619/592-0689
tgcrane@craneconsulting.com • www.craneconsulting.com

# Ordering Information

**FTA→**  FTA Press
11052 Picaza Place
San Diego, CA 92127
619/487-9017
Fax 619/592-0689

Please send _____ copies of *The Heart of Coaching* at $16.95 each. Add $4.50 Priority Mail postage and handling for the first book and 75¢ for each additional book. For books shipped to California addresses, please add California state sales tax.

Please charge my  ☐ Visa
                ☐ MasterCard  #: _____

Expiration date: _____  Signature: _____

Enclosed is my check for: _____

Name: _____

Address: _____

City, State, ZIP: _____

☐ This is a gift. Please send directly to:

Name: _____

Address: _____

City, State, ZIP: _____

☐ Autographed by the author

   Autographed to: _____